GLOBETROTTER™

The best of
BARCELONA

SUE BRYANT

NH
NEW
HOLLAND

G LOBETROTTER™

First edition published in 2002
by New Holland Publishers (UK) Ltd
London • Cape Town • Sydney • Auckland
10 9 8 7 6 5 4 3 2 1

website: www.newhollandpublishers.com

Garfield House, 86 Edgware Road
London W2 2EA
United Kingdom

80 McKenzie Street
Cape Town 8001
South Africa

14 Aquatic Drive
Frenchs Forest, NSW 2086
Australia

218 Lake Road
Northcote, Auckland
New Zealand

Distributed in the USA by
The Globe Pequot Press, Connecticut

ISBN 1 84330 290 X

Publishing Manager (UK): Simon Pooley
Publishing Manager (SA): John Loubser
Managing Editor: Thea Grobbelaar
DTP Cartographic Manager: Genené Hart
Editor: Thea Grobbelaar

Designer: Lellyn Creamer
Cover design: Lellyn Creamer, Nicole Engeler
Cartographer: Marisa Galloway
Proofreader: Jacqueline de Villiers

Reproduction by Resolution (Cape Town) and
Hirt & Carter (Pty) Ltd, Cape Town
Printed and bound in Hong Kong by Sing Cheong
Printing Co. Ltd.

Although every effort has been made to ensure
that this guide is up to date and current at time
of going to print, the Publisher accepts no
responsibility or liability for any loss, injury or
inconvenience incurred by readers or travellers
using this guide.

Acknowledgements:
The author wishes to thank the Hotel Rey Juan
Carlos I; the Hotel Arts; and for assistance with
research, Gretchen Thornburn. The publishers
wish to thank Turisme de Barcelona and
Transports Municipals de Barcelona SA for their
help in the preparation of this book.

Front Cover: *Gaudí's amazing Casà Batlló.*
Title Page: *Don Quixote addressing La Rambla.*

CONTENTS

MAKE THE MOST OF YOUR GUIDE

Reading these two pages will help you to get the most out of your guide and save you time when using it. Sites discussed in the text are cross-referenced with the cover maps – for example, the reference 'Map B–C3' refers to the Barri Gòtic Map (Map B), column C, row 3. Use the Map Plan below to quickly locate the map you need.

MAP PLAN

Outside Back Cover   Outside Front Cover

Inside Front Cover   Inside Back Cover

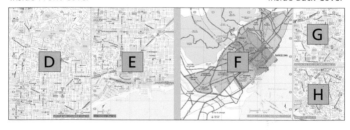

THE BIGGER PICTURE

Key to Map Plan

A – The Marina
B – Barri Gòtic
C – La Rambla
D – Gràcia and
     Eixample
E – La Ribera
F – Barcelona
     and Surrounds
G – Pedralbes
     and Les Corts
H – Montjuïc
I – Metro Map
J – Excursions

Key to Symbols

⊠ – address	⏱ – opening times
☎ – telephone	🚌 – tour
🕯 – fax	💰 – entry fee
💻 – website	🍴 – restaurants nearby
🖱 – e-mail address	M – nearest metro station

Map Legend

motorway	═══════	main road	Via Augusta
national road	━━━━━	pedestrian mall	C. DE PARADIS
main road	═══════	other road	C. de Sant Pau
river	*Llobregat*	built-up area	
route number	N340	post office	⊠
city	BARCELONA	parking area	P
major town	⊙ Manresa	police station	●
town	○ Sant Sadurní d'Anoia	hospital	⊕
village	◎ Tossa de Mar	building of interest	Temple Expiatori de la Sagrada Família
airport	✈	metro station	Ⓜ Liceu
peaks in metres	Montagut ▲ 964 m	commuter train (FGC)	Ⓕ Gràcia
place of interest	● *Museu Ceràmica*	place of worship	△ Santa Maria
railway	───────	tourist information	[i]
hotel	Ⓗ MAJESTIC	park & garden	*Parc del Migdia*

Keep us Current

Travel information is apt to change, which is why we regularly update our guides. We'd be most grateful to receive feedback from you if you've noted something we should include in our updates. If you have any new information, please share it with us by writing to the Publishing Manager, Globetrotter, at the office nearest to you (addresses on the imprint page of this guide). The most significant contribution to each new edition will be rewarded with a free copy of the updated guide.

Above: *A panoramic view of Barcelona from Mt Tibidabo.*

BARCELONA

Vibrant and chic, Barcelona is regarded as Spain's most exciting and cosmopolitan city. Situated on the **Mediterranean** between the golden beaches of the Costa Daurada to the south and the jagged cliffs and rocky coves of the Costa Brava to the north, Barcelona is the capital of **Catalunya**, one of Spain's most autonomous regions. While its roots go back over 2000 years to Carthaginian times, Barcelona today is a magnet to progressive thinkers and activists.

The Land
Climate

Barcelona enjoys a Mediterranean climate of hot summers, mild winters and extended spring and autumn seasons. The latter are the most conducive to wandering round the city, which is ideally suited to exploring on foot.

Plant Life

Barcelona has just one big park, the **Parc de la Ciutadella** (*see* page 19), with gardens, fountains and statues. The city's real green lung is **Mt Tibidabo**, cloaked in holm oaks and stone and aleppo pines. Other parks, Parc Güell and Parc Joan Miró, are more of a shrine to art and architecture than a celebration of nature, but an effort has been made to preserve native species like wild herbs, holm oaks and olives.

Wildlife

The best birdwatching is on the seafront, where migratory **birds** gather as they head south from June. At nearby Montserrat, you could spot wild boar, deer and genet cats while further afield, in the Pyrenees, birds of prey and larger **mammals** are more common.

History in Brief

The earliest known remains in Catalunya are dolmens or burial chambers dating back to 5000BC, found in the Pyrenees. By about 600BC Greek ships arrived and trading posts were established on what is now the Costa Brava. Around 300BC, Carthaginian troops came from what is now Tunisia, and the colony of **Barcino** was established. **Hannibal** crossed the Pyrenees in 214BC to invade Italy, but in the Second Punic War (218–201BC) the Carthaginians were expelled from Catalunya by the **Romans**, who settled the area. In 15BC **Emperor Augustus** officially named the city Julia Augusta Favencia Paterna Barcino.

In AD476 the **Visigoths** captured the city, naming their new territory *Gotalonia*. The Visigoths were ousted by the **Moors** in 713, who were in turn forced out by the **Franks** in 801. After Charlemagne's death, **Guifré el Pilos** (Wilfred the Hairy) appointed himself the first Count of Barcelona. In 988 **Borell II** declared Barcelona an autonomous region. **Ramón Berenguer I** (1035–76), a subsequent count, was the first to draw up the **Usatges de Barcelona**, a constitution for the new state.

Ferdinand and Isabella

A Castilian prince, **Ferdinand de Antequera**, was elected to the throne in 1412. In 1469 his great grandson, also Ferdinand, married Princess Isabella of Castile, uniting Castile and Catalunya-Aragón, Spain's two most powerful territories. When **Columbus** returned from the discovery of the New World in 1492, however,

> **Origins of Barcelona**
> Legends abound concerning the origins of the name Barcelona. One goes as far as to suggest that Hercules was the city's founding father. Another, more popular belief is that Hamilcar Barca, a rich Carthaginian and the father of the famous Hannibal, founded the settlement in 300BC and gave it the name Barcino. There is no evidence, however, to substantiate this, though Hannibal himself visited the city in 217BC.

Below: *Magnificent ships, such as this 16th-century royal barge in Barcelona's Maritime Museum, are a part of the city's heritage.*

Spain's attention began to turn away from the Mediterranean ports to those on the Atlantic. By 1494, Catalans had been replaced in positions of power by Castilians.

Independent Catalunya

Barcelona became increasingly impoverished till the **Thirty Years' War** with France. In 1635 Catalan rebels rose up against Castile, declaring Catalunya an independent republic.

Independence did not last. In 1714 the Bourbon King, Felipe V, took Barcelona on **11 September**, a day still remembered as a national holiday. In 1808 the city rose up against **Napoleon's** army in the Peninsular War. Napoleon and his men were eventually driven out of Spain by the British army.

The 20th Century

In 1914, the first Catalan provincial government was set up, only to be crushed by the dictatorship of **General Primo de Rivera**. A second republic was founded in 1931, but unrest was growing all over the country.

Spain's problems intensified and in July 1936 **General Francisco Franco** led an army uprising against the socialist government. Three years of bitter civil war followed. Over 600,000 lives were lost and entire towns were wiped out. Support from Italy and Germany led to Franco's victory in the civil war and in 1939 he proclaimed himself head of state of an exhausted, destitute Spain.

By the end of World War II, in which Spain remained neutral, the country was economically and politically isolated, and ostracized by the UN.

Before Franco died in 1975 he handed power over to **King Juan Carlos** who oversaw the transition to democracy and is today head of the constitutional monarchy and commander in chief of the armed forces.

Above: *King Juan Carlos and the royal family are highly respected in Spain.*
Opposite: *Cannons at Montjuïc castle are a reminder of the city's violent past.*

Government and Economy

In 1979 Catalunya received its statute of autonomy and Catalan was recognized as an official language. In 1982 the PSOE (**Socialist Workers' Party**), led by Felipe Gonzáles, was elected to power in Spain. The Socialist government integrated Spain into the European Community in 1986 and the country continued to prosper, putting itself in the spotlight in 1992, with the Sevilla **Expo**, the **Olympics** in Barcelona and **European City of Culture** in Madrid all in the same year. Jose Maria Aznar has been prime minister since 1996.

The Barcelona Olympics was the catalyst for over $2 billion of joint ventures between the public and private sectors. The inner city was renovated; new roads were built (including a four-lane ring road) and the port and rail links were upgraded. In a mission to shift Barcelona from secondary industry into the service sector, then mayor Pasqual Maragall encouraged heavy industry to move to the Zona Franca, the area between Montjuïc and the airport. Two new business districts have been created: the Carre Tarragona, location of car manufacturer SEAT's headquarters, and the area around the World Trade Centre on the seafront.

> **Josep Puig i Cadafalch**
> Catalan nationalist Josep Puig i Cadafalch (1867–1957) was president of the Catalan regional government from 1916 to 1923. He was also an art historian and architect, a disciple of Domènech i Montaner (see panel, page 12), although his work was more Gothic in style with lots of detailed floral decoration and some dramatic medieval influences, evident in the towers and turrets of the Casa de les Punxes on the Diagonal. One of his most visited works is Els Quatre Gats, the café in the Barri Gòtic where Picasso and his contemporaries would drink.

Above: *The game of* petanca *is highly popular among the older generation.*

The People

Catalan people are well known to be hard working and friendly, and a strong service ethic is evolving. Visitors may be surprised at the almost complete absence of any Spanish clichés like bullfighting, which has a lot of support in Madrid. In Barcelona football is the obsession and the team, FC Barcelona, enjoys hero status. The city is genuinely cosmopolitan, with a strong feminist movement and a thriving gay community.

Language

For over a thousand years, **Catalan**, a combination of Spanish, Latin and medieval French, has been spoken in Catalunya. The language in 12th-century Catalunya was almost identical to the *langue d'oc* spoken on the other side of the Pyrenees, and it quickly became the common trading language of the Mediterranean.

Catalan is still very widespread, and is also spoken in parts of Aragón, Andorra, certain areas of the Pyrenees and even southern Italy. The dialects of the Balearic Islands today are variations of Catalan rather than Castilian Spanish. The language looks strange to read and is not particularly easy to pronounce with its harsh, guttural sounds, but it can be mastered with some knowledge of French.

Throughout history, however, there have been attempts to suppress Catalan, most recently during **Franco's** dictatorship, in which books in Catalan were burned, and

<hr />

How to be a Local

You'll blend in with the local people if you try the following:
• Attend a football match at Camp Nou.
• Try to master the basics of Catalan.
• Don't expect your evening meal at 19:00 and don't even think of going to a nightclub before midnight.
• Use the metro and walk during the day.
• Explore the bars in Gràcia and, in summer, hang out at the Olympic Marina.
• Visit Maremagnum Centre on a Sunday.
• Try a *xampanyeria*, a bar specializing in *cava* (sparkling wine).
• Don't make remarks in favour of Madrid.

the language itself was banned on TV, the radio, in the press and was no longer taught in the schools.

Now, however, following a strong revival, Catalan has all but taken over from Castilian in Barcelona. Road signs, maps and advertising hoardings are all in Catalan. The language is spoken in offices, taxis and shops and in over half of all households. Almost everybody, however, is bilingual and visitors will always get by in Castilian.

Religion

Roman Catholicism is the dominant faith in Spain, although there is no state religion. Small pockets of **Protestantism** exist, and Barcelona also has a **synagogue** in Gràcia and two **mosques** in the city centre.

The Arts

Barcelona has some of the best modern collections in Europe – of graphic art, decorative art, ceramic art, contemporary art and textiles. The hub of the artistic community in the early 20th century was **Els Quatre Gats**, a bar where **Picasso**, **Ramón Casa** and **Pere Romeu** formed the nucleus of the crowd.

Art was suppressed during the civil war, but later, museums were opened to showcase the works of **Pablo Picasso**, **Joan Miró**, **Antoni Tàpies** and others. In Figueres, a couple of hours' drive north of Barcelona, the great surrealist **Salvador Dalí** opened a fine collection of his own in 1974.

> **Catalan Pronunciation**
> Catalan is mystifying to anyone who has just mastered basic Spanish as it's completely different, even though some words have a similar root. Here are a few of the more peculiar pronunciations:
> **g** followed by **e** or **i** is pronounced like the **zh** in Zhivago;
> **ig** is pronounced like **tch** in hatch;
> **n** before **f** or **v** is sometimes pronounced **m**;
> **r** is rolled at the beginning of a word and usually silent at the end;
> **v** at the beginning of a word is pronounced **b**, and **f** elsewhere;
> **w** is pronounced either **v** or **b**;
> **x** is pronounced **sh** in most words.

Below: *Residents of Gràcia admire the entries for an art competition.*

Opposite: *Parc Güell
is just one collection
of Antoni Gaudí's
bizarre designs.*
Below: *These
twisted chimney
stacks are typical
of Gaudí's style.*

Architecture

While Barcelona contains fine examples of
Gothic, Romanesque and Baroque architecture, it is the *modernista* work that people
flock to see. This developed in the early 20th
century as architects began to experiment
with new curves and floral ornamentation
on everything from the roof of a building to
its iron balconies and stained-glass windows.

The movement developed as Catalunya
was emerging from a long, dark depression
and Catalan nationalist feeling was strong.
Many architects wove this feeling into their
work and many buildings around Barcelona
are adorned with dragons and St George,
the patron saint of the city, and Catalan flag
emblems. The great **Antoni Gaudí** even in-
corporated Catalan birds and flowers into
his most famous work, the temple of the
Sagrada Família (*see* page 22).

Barcelona boasts 2000 listed buildings,
though regional towns also have their share
of gems. Look out for pavement designs,
lampposts and benches as well as houses, or
splashes of colour in a brilliant stained-glass
window. The city's most famous buildings are
the **Mansana de la Discòrdia** (*see* page 46),
three fantastical houses on the Passeig de
Gràcia; Gaudí's **La Pedrera** (*see* page 21) and
his **Sagrada Família** (*see*
page 22); Domènech i
Montaner's magnificent
concert hall, the **Palau de
la Música Catalana** (*see*
page 72); his **Castell dels
Tres Dragons** in Parc de la
Ciutadella, and the tiled
**Hospital de la Santa Creu i
de Sant Pau** (*see* page 36).

The second great architectural revival of the century came in the form of a massive facelift for the 1992 Olympic Games. Graceful buildings with clean lines were constructed, such as the **Palau de Sant Jordi** (*see* page 29) on Montjuïc and the two towers overlooking the **Olympic Marina** in the Vila Olimpica to the north of the Gothic Quarter.

Postmodernist parks such as the **Parc de l'Espanya Industrial** tried to make modern art an integral part of the city. Evoking the themes of light, space and simplicity are the Fundació Joan Miró on Montjuïc and the new **Museu d'Art Contemporani de Barcelona** (*see* page 37).

Antoni Gaudí (1852–1926)

Barcelona's most famous son, Antoni Gaudí, was sponsored from an early age by the wealthy **Güell family**, hence the names of many of his buildings – Palau Güell, Finca Güell and Parc Güell, for example. His earlier works, Casa Milà and Casa Batlló, were **expressionist** with their undulating forms and face-like features, but as **religion** came to play an important role in his life, Gaudí's designs, principally the Sagrada Família, contained more religious symbolism. Nature also had a huge influence on Gaudí's work. Sadly, in 1926, by which time he had become almost a recluse, living alone on the building site of the Sagrada Família on which he had been working since 1883, he was run over by a tram. Nobody recognized the tattered old man but when his identity became clear, the streets were packed for his funeral. The 150th anniversary of his birth, 2002, has been designated 'Gaudí Year' in Barcelona.

Designer Tombs

So popular and so fashionable was *modernista* that land had to be found for a new cemetery so that the upper classes could have space for specially commissioned, elaborate tombs. The southeast face of Montjuïc was chosen and the miniature temples and palaces are visible today from the new ring road that leads to the airport. Josep Vilaseca built a tomb for the Batlló family guarded by Egyptian-style angels, while Puig constructed mini-masterpieces for the Terrades family (who commissioned the turreted Casa de les Punxes) and the Barons of Quadres, whose former home on the Diagonal now houses the Museu de la Música.

Museu d'Art de Catalunya
🕐 10:00–19:00 Tue–Sat, 10:00–21:00 Thu, 10:00–14:30 Sun
✉ Palau Nacional, Parc de Montjuïc
☎ 93 423-7199, 622-0360 or 622-0360
🖷 93 325-5773 or 622-0374
💻 www.barcelona-on-line.es/eng/oci/museus_mnac.htm
💻 www.gencat.es/mnac/
M Espanya
🛋 Free entrance first Thursday of the month.

Below: *Cascading fountains in front of the Palau Nacional.*

⚙ *See* Map H–A1 ★★★

PALAU NACIONAL

The neoclassical Palau Nacional, constructed for the 1929 Expo, was supposed to have been dismantled in 1934 but a new use was found for it as home to one of the most impressive collections of medieval art in the world, now the **Museu d'Art de Catalunya**.

The Romanesque section of the museum consists of room after room of magnificent frescoes, all brought in from tiny churches dating back 1000 years and located high in the Pyrenees. The frescoes, mostly of biblical scenes, were removed for their protection around 1920, the reason being that the churches were lying abandoned. The best-known works include the apse from the church of Santa María de Taüll, with a scene of David and Goliath, and the 1123 masterpiece of Pantocràtor from Sant Climent de Taüll. An astonishing feature of these ancient frescoes is their brilliant colours.

The Gothic collection includes church pieces, tombs and paintings, representing the best of Catalan art with works by, among others, Jaume Huguet. The Spanish greats such as Velázquez and El Greco are represented in the later Baroque and Renaissance rooms.

Reaching the Palau Nacional has been made much easier now that giant escalators have been built on either side of the long flights of steps leading up to the building.

⊙ *See* Map H–B2   ★★★

FUNDACIÓ JOAN MIRÓ

One of Barcelona's best museums, the building of the Miró Foundation is as much a joy as the contents. The museum opened in 1975, though Miró formed the Joan Miró Foundation in 1971 with his friend, **Joan Prats**. It was a cultural venture with two objectives: to provide a centre for the study of Miró's work and to promote contemporary and avant-garde art.

There are two main sections. The **Miró section** features giant woven rugs in the stunning primary colours that were his trademark, and his paintings and drawings, which show a delight in colour and form. On the roof is a collection of his bizarre sculptures, displayed at their best in the sunlight. One of the most poignant exhibits, portraying the suffering during the civil war, is the Barcelona series from 1939–44: black and white lithographs on a yellow wall. Also here is Alexander Calder's **Mercury Fountain**, designed in 1937 for the Spanish government's pavilion at the Paris Expo. Calder described the work as 'an attempt to bring movement to sculpture'.

The second section, the '**To Joan Miró**' room, contains work donated by, among others, **Henry Moore**, **Matisse**, **Richard Serra**, **Antoni Tàpies**, and **Angel Ferrant**, all friends of the artist. Also fascinating is the room of Miró's sketches and life drawings – it is interesting to see the jottings on restaurant menus and bits of newspaper that became million-dollar masterpieces.

There's a pleasant café and a stylish souvenir shop at the complex. The foundation is an important centre for contemporary classical music and hosts a series of concerts in summer.

Above: *Joan Miró's metal sculptures are displayed on the flat roof of the Fundació Joan Miró to show off their dazzling colours.*

Fundació Joan Miró
🕐 10:00–19:00 Tue–Sat, 10:00–21:30 Thu, 10.00–14:30 Sun and public holidays
✉ Paseo de Miramar, s/n Parque de Montjuïc, 08038 Barcelona
☎ 93 443-9470 (museum)
☎ 93 329-0768 (restaurant)
📞 93 329-8609
🖷 fjmiro@bcn.fjmiro.es
🖳 www.bcn.fjmiro.es
M Paral.lel
♿ Special rate applies for groups of over 15 persons.
🍽 Restaurant with open-air terrace at the Foundation.

Below: *Beautiful old façades adorn the Plaça del Pi.*

⚘ *See* Map C   ★ ★ ★

LA RAMBLA

La Rambla (*see* pages 44–45) is a long promenade stretching from Plaça de Catalunya to the seafront. The name comes from the Arabic *ramla*, or torrent – it was once a seasonal stream running outside the city walls.

Rambla dels Flors, the most beautiful section, is lined with flower stalls: huge bunches of flowers clash brilliantly with one another in a riot of orange, pink, scarlet and electric blue. You can buy anything from a pet Venus flytrap to a bonsai tree or a cactus garden in a jar.

While it's tempting to lose oneself in the scents and colours of the flowers, a glance upward could reveal an artist's easel on a wrought-iron balcony, or a dusky pink-coloured façade with faded frescoes. Look down a side street and you may see a clown painting his face with a mournful smile, while buskers play haunting melodies on pan pipes and jugglers entertain the crowd.

Signposted from La Rambla, **Plaça del Pi** is a beautiful, shady square with a weekend market selling beeswax candles, mountain honey, goats' cheese and jars of quince jelly. The square is named after the pine tree at its centre, and orange trees, heavy with fruit in spring, provide shade in which to enjoy a *café con leche*. Dominated by the church of **Santa María del Pi** (*see* page 34), the square is always busy with buskers who make use of the excellent acoustics provided by the old houses and the stone of the church.

La Rambla
🖳 www.barcelona-on-line.es/eng/turisme/bcn_rambla.htm

Mercat de les Flors
🕘 09:00–21:00 Mon–Sat, 09:00–15:00 Sun
Ⓜ Liceu

Santa María del Pi
✉ Plaça del Pi 7, Ciutat Vella, Barri Gòtic
☎ 93 318-4743
Ⓜ Liceu

⭐ *See* Map B–B1 | ★ ★ ★

LA SEU
Catedral de Santa Eulàlia

La Seu is in the heart of the **Barri Gòtic**, facing Plaça de la Seu. Wherever you walk in the Gothic quarter, crammed among the alleys and jumble of palaces, the cathedral looms. The site was first a Roman temple and briefly, in Moorish times, a mosque.

Inside, the cathedral used to be dark and gloomy because the stained-glass windows are so high. Clever lighting, however, has given the building a sensation of space, its vaulted ceiling soaring high above the gilded chapels below. The cathedral is dedicated to **Santa Eulàlia**, the female patron saint of Barcelona. Her death and martyrdom in AD304 are illustrated on the 16th-century marble choir screen in the nave, by Ordóñez i Villar. A crypt below the altar contains her tomb. Around the edge of the cathedral are 29 chapels illuminated by candles. The most impressive tomb is that of Ramón Berenguer I, Count of Barcelona until 1025.

The **cloister** is quite a surprise. Tall palms and shady magnolias create a tropical garden in the most unlikely setting, completed by a gaggle of vociferous geese, apparently there to guard the tomb of Santa Eulàlia.

Just off the cloister is the small **Museu de la Catedral** containing Bartolomé Bermejo's stunning work *La Pietat* (The Devotion) and a 15th-century altarpiece by Catalan painter Huguet (1414–92).

La Seu
🕐 08:00–13:30 and 16:00–19:30 daily (cathedral), 11:00–13:00 daily (museum)
✉ Plaça de la Seu, 08002 Barcelona
☎ 93 315-1554 (cathedral)
☎ 93 310-2580 or 315-3555 (museum)
🖥 www.website.es/catedralbcn (cathedral)
🖥 www.barcelona-online.es/eng/oci/museus_catedral.htm (museum)
Ⓜ Jaume I
ⓘ Admission to the cathedral is free, but there is an entry fee for the museum.

Below: *Bright sunlight streams through the graceful arches in the cloisters of La Seu.*

Museu Picasso
🕐 10:00–20:00 Tue–
Sat, 10:00–15:00 Sun
✉ Carrer Montcada
15–19, 08003
Barcelona
☎ 93 319-6310 or
315-4761
📠 93 315-0102
🖥 www.barcelona-on-
line.es/eng/oci/museus_
picasso.htmv
M Jaume I
🔥 Free entrance first
Sunday of the month.

⬙ See Map E–A3	★★★

MUSEU PICASSO

Housed in three medieval palaces, the Picasso Museum is laid out in a series of rooms representing different phases of the artist's life. The huge variation in style illustrates his incredible talent and diversity. The museum owns 3000 of Picasso's works, of which about 500 are on display. The initial collection was donated by Picasso's friend and one-time secretary Jaime Sabartes in 1963 and added to by the artist himself after Sabartes's death in 1968.

If you can understand Spanish and Catalan instructions, follow the rooms in chronological order. Picasso's early works consist of tiny sketches and studies and some portraits painted in his youth. There are scenes of the city, including a watercolour of Barceloneta in 1897, when it was just a tiny fishing village.

Below: *The Picasso Museum is housed in a series of medieval palaces.*

Examples from Picasso's various periods follow, with collections from his **Blue Period** (1901–04), **Pink Period** (1904–06) and later Cubist and neoclassical phases. Some of the most spectacular paintings are from 1957, dazzling blues and acid greens of his time in Cannes, the study of the Velázquez masterpiece, *Las Meninas,* and the scarlet-and-lime of his portraits of his wife Jacqueline, which occupy five rooms. Don't miss the ceramics; 41 pieces were donated to the museum by Jacqueline in 1981.

The museum has a research **library** boasting an array of comprehensive books, as well as a charming café and a shop selling prints of virtually everything in the museum.

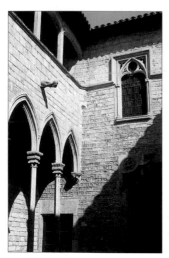

See Map E–B4 ★★★

PARC DE LA CIUTADELLA

Below: *The park gives city dwellers vital green space.*

Barcelona is strangely lacking in green spaces. Areas of the Eixample allocated for parkland were soon developed as the city grew. Green areas were created in 1992 for the Olympics but till then, Montjuïc, Parc Güell and Parc de la Ciutadella were the only areas where people could jog and walk their dogs. The latter is named after a citadel built by Felipe V in 1715 to keep the city under control after it resisted his cause in the War of Spanish Succession. Much of the citadel was destroyed in 1869 to make way for a park and what remains of the Baroque palace is now the seat of the Catalan parliament and the **Museum of Modern Art** (not to be confused with the Museum of Contemporary Art).

Scattered around the park is an eclectic collection of buildings designed for the 1888 Universal Exposition. A vast **Arc de Triomf**, a mock-*Mudéjar* arch by Josep Vilaseca, served as the entrance to the Expo. The best feature is the outrageous **Cascada** fountain, designed by Josep Fontserè with assistance from the young Gaudí. Now overgrown with moss and creepers, this mock-Baroque extravaganza is topped with winged lions and dramatic horse-drawn chariots, with fiery dragons jutting out below.

The park also houses the **Parc Zoològic de Barcelona** (the city zoo), as well as both the Zoological and Geological museums.

Museu d'Art Modern de Catalunya
🕐 10:00–19:00 Tue–Sat, 10:00–14:30 Sun and public holidays.
☎ 93 319-5728
📠 93 319-5965
✆ mnac@correu.gencat.es
🖳 www.bcn.es/english/turisme/itinerar/ciutadel/imartmdr.htm
Ⓜ Ciutadella Vila Olímpica

Parc Zoològic
🕐 10:00–17:00 year-round, with extended hours in summer.
☎ 93 225-6780
📠 93 221-3853
🖳 www.zoobarcelona.com (zoo)
🖳 www.bcn.es/english/turisme/itinerar/ciutadel/iciutade.htm (park)
Ⓜ Ciutadella Vila Olímpica
🚌 Guided tours of the zoo are run by the Department of Education; contact them on ☎ 93 225-6787.

Below: *Casa Batlló's roof tiles resemble a dragon's scales.*

🟢 See Map D–A6	★★★

CASA BATLLÓ

The interpretation of St George and the Dragon is more dramatic than usual in **Gaudí's** fabulous Casa Batlló, where he added a new façade to an existing building owned by industrialist **Josep Batlló**. The whole building has striking dragon-like qualities; bright turquoise, brown and green mosaics make up the façade, and the roof undulates like a scaly dragon's back. Concrete almost appears to drip from the overhanging ledges like folds of skin. Window frames resemble bleached bones, presumably of the dragon's victims, while the iron balconies stare like malevolent eyes or animal skulls. On the roof, the cross-shaped chimney represents the sword of **St George** piercing the dragon's back.

This bizarre design continues inside – the lobby has a lizard-skin motif, painstakingly painted onto the atrium walls. The concierge sits in a kind of cave and staircases disappear in stone tunnels down to the basement. Even the tiny windows have a scaly pattern. The building is privately owned and can be rented out for corporate cocktail parties. It opened to the public for the first time in 2002 (from March to October) as part of the celebration of Gaudí Year (*see* page 13).

Casa Batlló
🕐 09:00–14:00 daily
✉ Passeig de Gràcia 43, Eixample
☎ 93 216-0366
for information and pre-booking
☎ 93 488-0666
📠 93 488-3090
🖥 informacion@ casabatllo.es
🖳 www.casabatllo.es
Ⓜ Passeig de Gràcia

See Map D–A5	★★★

LA PEDRERA

Casa Milà, as it is correctly known, is one of Gaudí's most impressive creations – a huge apartment building that covers a whole block, its roughly finished stone exterior moulded and rounded to resemble cave dwellings. This rock-like appearance gave the building its name, **La Pedrera**, which means 'the quarry'. The wrought iron balconies form strange, organic shapes and the twisted chimney stacks, which stand out emphatically among the surrounding buildings, look remarkably like human forms. Apartments in the building are highly prized.

Tours of the building are conducted in a variety of languages (*see* information panel, above right). On summer evenings the roof terrace opens as a bar, and there is live music on Saturdays and Sundays.

La Pedrera
🕐 10:00–20:00 daily, 10:00–15:00 holidays
✉ Passeig de Gràcia 92, on corner of carrer de Provença
☎ 93 484-5980
💻 www.op.net/ ~jmeltzer/Gaudi/mila. html
M Diagonal
🚌 Tours at 11:00, 12:00, 13:00, 16:00 and 17:00 Mon–Fri, 10:00, 11:00 and 12:00 Sat–Sun.

Gaudí
For all his glory in his native town, Gaudí's work is hardly featured outside Catalunya. He has, however, produced a few works in other parts of Spain. In 1903 he was commissioned to restructure the interior of the magnificent cathedral in Palma. In Santander, he designed a country house with a minaret-like circular tower for the brother-in-law of the Marquis of Comillas. There are two Gaudí buildings in Leon: a house designed for Güell's friends, and a spectacular Bishop's Palace in Astorga, which looks like a small castle.

Left: *Gaudí's Casa Milà, known as La Pedrera, is a landmark in Eixample.*

See Map D–C5 ★★★

Sagrada Família
🕐 09:00–20:00 daily (church), 10:00–14:00 and 16:00–19:00 daily (museum)
✉ Mallorca 401, Plaza de la Sagrada Família
☎ 93 207-3031 or 455-0247
📠 93 435-8335 or 476-1010
✉ sagfam@grupart.es
🖥 www.sagradafamilia. org/eng/principal.htm
🖥 www.gaudiclub.com
🖥 www.sagfam/ deakin/edu/au
M Sagrada Família
💰 Different rates for individuals, groups of more than 10 people, young and retired people, pupils; under 10s have free entry.
🚌 *see page 49.*

SAGRADA FAMÍLIA
Temple Expiatori de la Sagrada Família

This is probably Barcelona's most famous landmark and Gaudí's best-known artistic work. Though half-built, it is awe-inspiring. Soaring spires are topped with brilliant colours, concrete drips like icicles from a façade of clouds, and giant inscriptions of 'Sanctus Sanctus Sanctus' encircle the spires.

A religious group, the Associació de Devots de Sant Josep, wanted a cathedral for the poor of the growing city. They commissioned architect Francesc de Paula Villar i Lozano and the church was begun in 1882. Villar was replaced by Gaudí who, becoming increasingly devout, proposed to build a symbol of the city, bringing together all his previous interpretations of nature in architecture.

Gaudí lived and worked on the site until his death in 1926, by which time the crypt, part of the apse, the **Nativity Façade** (*see page 34*) and one tower were finished. His tomb lies in the crypt. Though many of the plans were destroyed in the civil war, enough remained to continue the work in 1957. The present towers were finished in 1975. Today construction continues amid controversy. One faction believes the project should be left as it is, in tribute to Gaudí, while others are determined to see it completed.

Under the site, the **Museu de la Sagrada Família** follows the history of the building and explains the method behind Gaudí's work.

Below: *Cranes are interspersed with the graceful spires of the unfinished Sagrada Família.*

See Map D–C2 ★★★

PARC GÜELL

This city oasis was intended to be an exclusive housing estate. Güell bought the land on the slopes of the **Muntanya Pelada** in 1899 and commissioned Gaudí to design 60 houses with gardens, but only two were built. Today the park is protected by UNESCO as a world heritage site. It was declared a historical monument in 1969 and the only remaining house is now the **Casa Museu Gaudí**, which was founded by the Friends of Gaudí in 1963.

The most striking feature of the park is the marketplace. Two pavilions flank the park's entrance, and a flight of steps – guarded by a large, colourful dragon – leads up to a market square. Underneath, 86 columns create a gallery effect where the market stalls would have been, but today it is curiously empty. White, broken mosaic patterns across a contoured ceiling give the impression of billowing clouds.

On top is the amazing **wave bench**, a continuous, undulating stone bench decked in mosaic. Barcelona stretches out below, and at weekends the place is packed. Higher up are children's play areas facing west to Tibidado and a small *petanca* square where old men gather for a heated debate over the game.

In the centre of the park is the **Casa Museu Gaudí**. Gaudí did not actually design this house but he lived here from 1906 to 1926. Inside, the house is disappointingly austere; Gaudí was deeply religious and lived a spartan life. There are, however, a few *modernista* gems, a mirror with an elaborate gilt frame, a few pieces of furniture and some extravagant fabric samples.

Above: *Locals gather to read the Sunday papers on Gaudí's wave bench.*

Parc Güell
🕐 10:00–14:00 and 16:00–19:00 Mon–Fri, 10:00–14:00 Sun
✉ Casa d'Olot, Barcelona
☎ 93 414-6446, 219-3811, 284-6446 or 424-3809
🖥 www.op.net/ ~jmeltzer/Gaudi/ parkgell.html
M Plaça des Lesseps
💲 There are reductions for students, retired people and groups of more than 10.
🍴 There are cafés inside the park.

☼ *See* Map F–C2   ★★★

Above: *Barcelona's antique, but pristine, blue tram ferries visitors to the Tibidabo funicular.*

TIBIDABO

The highest point of the pine-clad hills that encircle the city is Mt Tibidabo, at a towering 550m (1805ft), from which the views are legendary. On a rare pollution-free day with the right atmospheric conditions, people claim to be able to see as far as the Balearic Islands, some 128km (80 miles) out to sea.

At weekends, local people flock to the hills to visit the excellent **amusement park** on Tibidabo (*see* page 40), have a picnic and enjoy the fresh air. Getting there by public transport is an adventure in itself. From the Plaça de Catalunya, take the FGC train to the Tibidabo stop. The heart of a rich suburb, its broad streets are lined with noblemen's houses built at the turn of the century, when Barcelona was expanding.

An antique tram, the **Tramvia Blau**, creaks and grinds its way up the hill to the Tibidabo funicular, smartly decked out in shiny, navy blue paint and highly polished wood. Look at the building on the corner by the tram stop, **La Rotunda**, an amazingly fussy *modernista* structure with a domed roof. Once a dance hall and brothel, it now serves as a hospital.

From the top of the tram line, take the funicular up the mountainside. At the top, there is a whole new world of entertainment as well as a couple of bars and restaurants with outdoor terraces offering a marvellous bird's-eye view of the city.

Parc d'Atraccions del Tibidabo
🕒 open weekends and holidays throughout the year
✉ Pl. Tibidabo 3–4, 08035 Barcelona
☎ 93 211-7942
📠 93 211-2111
🖥 www.barcelona turisme.com/turisme/exp/ing/ap07-54.htm

TIBIDABO & MONTSERRAT

☆ See Map J–C1 | ★★★

MONTSERRAT

Montserrat is shrouded in legend and mystery. The mountain itself is incredibly beautiful, rising up from the plain like a row of jagged teeth. The monastery is cut into the rock, sheltered by wind- and rain-blasted limestone towers.

A thousand years ago, hermits lived in huts and caves on the mountain because it was supposed to be a holy place, once visited by St Peter who left an icon of the Virgin Mary in a cave. There is indeed a statue, **La Moreneta** – an unusual carving with a black face and hands. Legend has it that the icon went missing during the Moorish invasion of the 8th century, only to reappear in the late 9th century. A shrine was built around the statue, but in the 12th century it was replaced by a Romanesque building, part of which still stands today. The Virgin of Montserrat became the patron saint of Catalunya and her fame spread far and wide.

The monastery has suffered over the last 200 years. When Napoleon's forces invaded Catalunya in 1811, the hermits were driven off or killed and the monastery, filled with the most amazing wealth, was sacked and partly destroyed. What is left of the building today is a mixture of late 16th-century Gothic and Modern (19th-century) styles.

Montserrat is one of Catalunya's most important tourist attractions (*see page 82*), for its spectacular mountain scenery as much as for its religious significance. In addition to thousands of tourists and pilgrims, hundreds of newlyweds (many of whom are staunch Catholics) also make the pilgrimage here.

Montserrat Monastery
Location: about 80km (50 miles) from the city centre, an hour by train
🖥 www.virtourist.com/ europe/montserrat/

Museu de Montserrat
🕐 10:30– 14:00 and 15:00–18:00
☎ 93 835-0251
📠 93 828-4049

Below: *Montserrat's monastery perches high on the mountainside, carved into sheer rock.*

25

See Map J–F1 ★ ★ ★

Figueres
Location: about 200km (125 miles) from the city centre
🖥 www.dali-estate. org/eng/teatre.htm
🚌 Guided tours to Dalí's former home in Port Lligat are arranged by appointment for a nominal fee.

Dalí Museum
🕐 9:00–19:15 Jul–Sep, 10:30–17:15 Oct–Jun
✉ Plaza de Salvador Dalí y Gala s/n, Figueres
☎ 972 50-5697
📠 972 50-1666

FIGUERES

The main reason to visit the inland provincial town of Figueres is to see the amazing **Dalí Museum**, the most visited museum in Spain after the Prado in Madrid – even more popular than the Picasso Museum in Barcelona.

Dalí opened the museum in 1974, converting a former municipal theatre, a 19th-century building that had burned down in the civil war and fallen into decay. Today the museum is quite a sight; red, fortress-like walls topped with giant eggs and a huge dome, with the eerie **Torre Galatea**, where the artist spent his dying years, attached to one side of it. Inside, a sculpture garden has replaced the theatre stalls and a series of rooms contains increasingly bizarre works, including *Rainy Taxi*, whereby water sprays into a Cadillac when coins are inserted. Well-known works on the ground floor include *Soft Self Portrait with a Slice of Grilled Bacon* and *Portrait of Picasso*. Where the stage once was is a backdrop for a ballet, *Labyrinth*, and a portrait of Dalí's wife, Gala. On the first floor, visit the **Wind Palace Room** where there's a large fresco of two figures pouring gold coins through drawers onto the plain below.

The narrow streets and squares around the museum are lined with coffee shops, bars and shops selling every permutation of Dalí's works, from T-shirts to mugs, playing cards and pencil sharpeners.

Below: *The Dalí Museum in Figueres is the second most visited in Spain.*

See Map C–B3 | ★★

Below: *La Boquería is the city's best source of fresh produce.*

LA BOQUERÍA
Mercat Sant Josep

A tall iron gate on the west side of La Rambla (*see* page 16) marks the entrance to La Boquería, Barcelona's biggest and best-known **market**. Built between 1840 and 1870, this cavernous hall resembles a railway station and is a hive of activity from dawn onwards, as stallholders set out their wares in competition with one another. Enormous piles of brilliantly coloured vegetables and fruit, tables stacked high with pungent cheeses and long strings of plump, spicy sausages, not to mention huge displays of glistening fish, fresh from the morning's catch, make the market a wonderful place to browse around.

Shopping in markets in Barcelona is part of the city's culture and everyone, from professional chefs to office workers, frequents La Boquería. There are many other markets in the city (*see* pages 52–53), including Plaça del Pi off La Rambla, with an antique market on a Thursday and a honey market on the first Friday and Saturday of the month. Plaça Sant Josep Oriol has an art market every weekend, and coins and stamps are traded in the Plaça Reial on Sundays. There's also a craft market in Gràcia (Avinguda Pau Casals) on the first Sunday of the month.

La Boquería
🕐 08:00–20:30 Mon–Sat
✉ La Rambla 91, 08002 Barcelona
☎ 93 318-2584
🖥 www.bcn.es/english/barcelon/compres/imercat1.htm
M Liceu
🍽 Bar Pinotxo, inside the market hall.

Below: *The lavish interior of Gaudí's Palau Güell.*

 See Map C–A5   ★★

PALAU GÜELL

On the west side of La Rambla is one of Antoni Gaudí's early *modernista* works, the Palau Güell. Built in 1885 for Don Eusebio Güell, a wealthy shipowner, it now houses the **Theatre Museum**. Some notable features include the vast, heavy balcony over the entrance with its intricate iron work and the bizarre, twisted chimney stacks covered with colourful tiles, a Gaudí trademark. Inside, his influence is visible in the undulating columns and archways.

The shipowner and industrialist **Eusebio Güell** (1846–1918) was Gaudí's main patron from 1878, when they met, until 1918 when Güell died at the age of 71. Güell commissioned some of Gaudí's most important works, including the Palau Güell and the Parc Güell, intended by the patron to be an exclusive housing estate but in the end inhabited only by himself and Gaudí. Güell was such an admirer of Gaudí's work that he arranged a special exhibition of the architect's achievement in Paris in 1910. The exhibition was a success although Gaudí failed to attend, having by now virtually become a depressive recluse because of his obsession with building the Sagrada Família Cathedral.

Palau Güell
🕐 10:00–13:30 and 16:00–19:30 Mon–Sat (palace)
🕐 11:00–14:00 and 17:00–20:00 Tue–Sat (museum)
✉ Nou de la Rambla 3
☎ 93 301-7775 or 317-3974 (palace)
☎ 93 317-5198 (museum)
🖥 www.op.net/ ~jmeltzer/gaudi.html
M Liceu or Drassanes
🚌 Guided tours, sometimes in English, are available.

See Map H–A2 | ★★

OLYMPIC STADIUM

Barcelona's Olympic Stadium is perched high on the rocky mass of Montjuïc with the city and the Mediterranean stretched out below. The stadium was constructed for the 1929 Expo and was intended to be used for the 'people's' alternative to the Nazi-dominated 1936 Olympics in Berlin. These never, in fact, took place as the Spanish Civil War broke out before the stadium was even opened.

New Catalan architects were brought in to modernize the stadium for the 1992 Games, although the 1929 façade was retained. To create a classical-style stadium, the arena's original base was sunk 12m (39ft) into the ground to accommodate 65,000 spectators.

In contrast to the neoclassical grandeur of the stadium, Japanese architect Arata Isozaki's **Palau de Sant Jordi** is a sleek, low-lying dome in silver and black. Holding 17,000 spectators, it is one of the largest sports halls in the world. The stone-and-metal 'forest' sculpture outside is the work of the architect's wife, Aiko Miyawaki.

At the south gate of the stadium, the **Galleria Olimpica** museum features some video footage from the 1992 Olympic Games as well as memorabilia from the games where a number of world records were set. For true Olympic fans, there are also a library and an information centre.

Olympic Stadium
10:00–14:00 and 16:00–20:00 Tue–Sat, 10:00–14:00 Sun (museum)
Pg Olímpic 17–19, Montjuïc, 08038 Barcelona
☎ 93 426-2089 (stadium)
☎ 93 426-0660 (museum)
www.bcn.es/english/turisme/perdis/ibcnolim. htm
M Espanya
Free tours take place between 10:00 and 18:00 daily.

Below: *Although modernized in 1992, the Olympic Stadium retains its original 1929 façade.*

See Map D ★★

Casa Vicens
⏱ Not open to the public.
✉ 24–26 Carrer de Les Carolines
🖥 www.op.net/ ~jmeltzer/Gaudi/vicens. html
M Lesseps, Fontana

GRÀCIA

Once a small village on the plains, Gràcia has been swallowed up by the tentacles of the city. Home of the liberal and artistic community in the last century, Gràcia retains a village atmosphere and an independent spirit, especially during festivals when garlands deck the streets. Some of the city's best restaurants and bars are found here and a trip on a summer's night is most rewarding.

There are a few sights in Gràcia, notably **Casa Vicens**, one of Gaudí's first designs, built for a tile maker in 1883. Unlike Gaudí's later work, the house is geometric in design with strong _Mudéjar_ influences, and orange and blue tiles adorn the exterior.

Below: _Plaça del Sol is the main meeting place in Gràcia._

In the heart of Gràcia, in the tower of Plaça de Ruis i Taulet, is the **Campana de Gràcia** – the Gràcia bell. In 1870, during a revolt against taxes, the bell was tolled incessantly and could be heard in Barcelona.

Another place that is worth stopping for is the **Plaça del Sol**, which is packed with life on a hot summer's night as locals gather at the outside tables for a drink before moving on to Gràcia's many clubs and restaurants. By day, the square is a great spot for people watching.

See Map G–B1 | ★★

Below: *Medieval walls on Pedralbes's ancient monastery.*

MONASTIR DE PEDRALBES

This beautiful Gothic monastery is located at the further end of Avinguda Pedralbes, near the Collserola hills. Consisting of a cluster of medieval buildings in a good state of repair, the monastery was founded in 1326 by **Queen Elisenda de Montcada**, the last wife of **King Jaume II**. Nuns of the order of St Clare have lived here since the 14th century and a wander through the old refectory (the communal dining hall), kitchens and herb garden gives a fascinating insight into their lives.

The **cloisters**, however, are the monastery's most exquisite feature – three levels of passageways supported by impossibly slender columns, with a Renaissance fountain at the centre. Frescoes and religious artefacts are stored in the gallery around the cloister.

The church dates back to 1419 and contains the marble tomb of Queen Elisenda, who lived here for the last 30 years of her life. The church is very simple in design, with a single aisle, and still retains some of its original stained-glass windows. There's also a small chapel, dedicated to Sant Miquel, which is decorated with ornate paintings from around 1345 by the Catalan artist Ferrer Bassa.

Monastir de Pedralbes
🕐 10.00–17:00 Tue–Sat, 10:00–14:00 Sun
✉ Baixada Monestir 9, 08034 Barcelona
☎ 93 280-1434
📠 93 203-9908
🖥 www.barcelona-on-line.es/eng/oci/museus_monestir.htm
M Maria Cristina
♿ Free entrance for under 12s.

See Map G–A3 ★

MUSEU DE FUTBOL CLUB BARCELONA

Above right: *FC Barcelona trophies are on display in the Football Museum.*

The district known as Les Corts was the scene of extensive building before the Olympics. The **Camp Nou** football stadium (home of the legendary **FC Barcelona**) is located here, as is the **Football Museum**.

Even the most reluctant visitor will recognize some of the names in this museum's hall of fame, which includes England's Gary Lineker and Argentina's Maradona. It is set inside the vast Camp Nou football stadium, which, with a capacity of 120,000, dwarfs the Olympic Stadium. The museum charts the history of Spain's most famous team, FC Barcelona, over the last century. A tour of the museum includes a visit to the VIP box, from which it is possible to appreciate the sheer size of the stadium. Matches take place most Sundays and while tickets are like gold dust they are worth fighting for to experience the spectacle of 120,000 roaring fans.

See Map A	★

THE SEAFRONT

Barcelona's run-down seafront was completely transformed for the 1992 Olympic Games. Crumbling docks were turned into glamorous yacht marinas, and a new promenade, **Moll de la Fusta** (once a timber wharf), now connects the Columbus statue to the eastern corner of the Barri Gòtic. A smart shopping mall, **Maremagnum**, with restaurants, an aquarium and an IMAX cinema, overlooks a bustling yacht marina enclosed by a small drawbridge. From just below the Columbus Monument, small passenger boats leave on half-hourly sightseeing tours of the harbour. The strange metal towers are not part of the docks; they are in fact stations for the panoramic cable car which makes the descent from Montjuïc across the harbour to the old fishing village of **Barceloneta**.

The **Columbus Monument**, a 50m (164ft) tall tower and a city landmark, was designed by Gaietà Buiges in 1886 for the 1888 Expo. Columbus perches on top, pointing out to sea. He was received in Barcelona in 1493 by the Catholic King and Queen, Ferdinand and Isabella, on his return from his first voyage to the New World. A somewhat cramped lift in the tower whisks passengers to the top for sweeping views across the city and docks, though the scratched Perspex windows make photography difficult.

Seafront
🕐 09:00–20:30 daily (monument), 12:00–19:00 daily in fine weather (cable car)
☎ 93 221-1499 (Centre Municipal de Vela in Port Olimpic, for sailing)
🖳 www.barcelona-on-line.es/eng/turisme/bcn_mar.htm
M Drassanes

Maremagnum Centre
✉ Odisea 2000 S.L. Unipersonal, Moll d'Espanya s/n, 08039 Barcelona
☎ 93 225-8100
📠 93 225-8096
🖅 maremagnum@maremagnum.es

Below: *Passenger boats depart from near the Columbus Monument for sightseeing tours of the waterfront.*

Above: *People, birds and animals form the detail of the Nativity Façade of Sagrada Família.*

Sagrada Família Landmarks

1890 First designs.
1925 The bell tower of St Barnabus is completed.
1926 The death of Antoni Gaudí.
1936 The church is desecrated during the Civil War.
1940 The crypt is restored.
1954 The Passion façade is constructed.
1977 The bell towers on the Passion façade are completed.
1995 The vaults on the side aisles are constructed.
From 2001 Sculptor Josep Maria Subirachs in charge of design, receiving criticism from Gaudí followers for straying too far from Gaudí's original ideas.

Churches and Cathedrals

Sagrada Família

Gaudí wanted the Nativity Façade of Sagrada Família (*see page 22*) to face east, so that the sunrise would bring new life to the miracle of birth every morning. Biblical scenes, from the coronation of the Virgin to the appearance of the angel Gabriel, are depicted. The caves, clouds and ice were all inspired by the rock formations at Montserrat (*see page 25*).

✉ *Mallorca 401, Plaza de la Sagrada Família,* ☎ *93 207-3031 or 455-0247,* 🖷 *93 435-8335,* **M** *Sagrada Família,* 🕓 *09:00–20:00 (church), 10:00–14:00 and 16:00–19:00 (museum).*

La Seu

For details and information, *see page 17.*
✉ *Plaça de la Seu, 08002 Barcelona,* ☎ *93 315-1554,* **M** *Jaume I,* 🕓 *07:00–13:30 and 16:00–19:30 daily (cathedral), 11:00–13:00 daily (museum).*

Santa María del Pi

Built in the 14th century, burned badly in the civil war of 1936 and restored in the 1960s, this church is Gothic in style. Rather austere on the outside, the interior is stunning, with a massive rose window throwing coloured sunbeams across the cool flagstones.
✉ *Plaça del Pi 7, Ciutat Vella, Barri Gòtic,* ☎ *93 318-4743,* **M** *Liceu.*

Sant Pau de Camp

This magnificent Catalan Romanesque church was once a Benedictine abbey. The naive carvings above the door date all the way back to the 13th century.
✉ *Carrer Sant Pau 101, Ciutat Vella, El Raval,* ☎ *93 441-0001,* 🕓 *the most sensible time to visit would be between 17:00 and 19:00, before evening mass; other services are 08:00 on weekdays and four times on Sunday.*

Sants Just i Pastor

This is supposedly Barcelona's oldest church, although most of the building dates from the 14th century. It was once the parish church for the Count-Kings of Barcelona and Aragón. Today the beautiful stained glass and intricate stone inside make the church a popular spot for weddings.

✉ *Plaça Sant Just 6, Ciutat Vella, Barri Gòtic,* ☎ *93 301-7433,* Ⓜ *Jaume I.*

Santa María del Mar

Built in 1323 by architect Berenguer de Montagut on what was then the seafront, this church is considered to be one of the best examples of Gothic Catalan architecture, because of the purity of its lines. The interior is very simple, with jewel-like stained-glass windows.

✉ *Plaça Santa María 1, Ciutat Vella, Parc,* ☎ *93 310-2390,* Ⓜ *Jaume I.*

El Sagrat Cor de Jesus

The two parts of this church, designed by Enric Sagnier, are almost like two separate buildings. A neo-Romanesque nave with some extravagant *modernista* features forms the base of this church, while the section above is neo-Gothic. It is topped by a statue of Christ, arms outstretched like the famous statue in Rio de Janeiro.

✉ *Pere IV, 398, Sant Martí, Poble Nou,* ☎ *93 307-1417,* ⏰ *08:00–19:00 daily.*

Above: *The lavish Sagrat Cor church is a popular venue for weddings.*
Below: *Stained-glass windows adorn the Santa María del Mar.*

Finca Güell

Beyond the palace is a large, grassy park, the **Parc de Pedralbes**, with Barcelona's University buildings on its fringes. At the far end of the park is the **Finca Güell**, the former stables of the wealthy Güell family, whose land stretched from here some distance south of the Diagonal. Gaudí was commissioned to build the porter's house, the gate and the stable pavilions, which are decked out in bright blue and white tiles. The only part of the estate visible to the public is the wrought-iron gate with its menacing dragon, which raises its claws when the gate is opened.

Below: *Typical of Catalan Gothic style, La Llotja houses the city's stock exchange.*

Historic Buildings
La Llotja

This building once housed the Consolat de Mar, which regulated sea traffic. It is now home to Barcelona's stock exchange. The building contains wide arches around a central courtyard, typical of Catalan Gothic architecture. The exterior is more recent, renovated in the late 18th century. Graceful, white marble statues adorn the neoclassical façade and roof.

⊠ *carrer del Consolat del Mar, Ciutat Vella, Parc,* ☎ *93 401-3555,* ✆ *93 401-3625,* **M** *Barceloneta.*

Hospital de la Santa Creu i de Sant Pau

The unique University Hospital, built by Domènech i Montaner, is a series of pavilions clad in colourful ceramics and domes. It is set in tranquil gardens. ⊠ *carrer de St Antoni Maria Claret 167, Horta-Guinardó,* ☎ *93 291-9191 or 291-9000,* **M** *Hospital de Sant Pau.*

Palau Reial de Pedralbes

Barcelona's Royal Palace is surrounded by gardens with pools and statues. It was built by extending a stately home belonging to the Güell family. Inevitably, Franco used it during the civil war. ⊠ *Avinguda Diagonal 686, Les Corts, Pedralbes,* ☎ *93 280-1964,* **M** *Palau Reial,* ⊕ *10:00–18:00 daily in winter, 10:00–20:00 in summer.*

Other interesting buildings on pages 20, 21 and 28.)

Museums and Galleries

Museu d'Art Contemporani de Barcelona

This futuristic museum has stark white walls, glossy black floors, glass and granite to offset over 1000 works by Calder, Miró and Klee (among others). Richard Meier, the building's architect, describes it as 'a cathedral of our time'.

✉ Plaça dels Angels 1, Ciutat Vella, El Raval,
☎ 93 412-0810,
📧 macba@macba.es
🖥 www.macba.es
M Universitat, 🕑 June–Sept 11:00–20:00 Mon, Wed, Fri; 11:00–21:00 Thurs; 10:00–20:00 Sat and 10:00–15:00 Sun. Oct–May 11:00–19:30 Mon, Wed, Fri; 11:00–20:00 Sat and 10:00–15:00 Sun.

Museu Maritim

The stone-vaulted ceilings of this museum protect a fine copy of a 16th-century royal barge (see page 7) and countless smaller vessels. Maps, compasses and special effects of storms and battles add to the atmosphere. A raised catwalk allows you to admire the interior roof structure and see the exhibits from a different angle.

✉ Av. Drassanes 1, Ciutat Vella, El Raval,
☎ 93 342-9920,
📧 m.barcelona@diba.es
📧 c.drassanes@diba.es
🖥 www.diba.es/mmaritim
M Drassanes,
🕑 10:00–13:30 and 16:00–19:30 Mon– Fri, 10:00–13:30 and 16:30–20:00 Sat, Sun and holidays.

Museu d'Història de la Ciutat

Palau Clariana Padellas has an unusual history. Originally on the carrer de Mercaders, the Palace was in the way of a proposed new road and in 1931 was moved to Plaça del Rei, where it was rebuilt over ancient remains. Exhibits include a 14th-century Christian basilica and parts of the city's 11th-century Romanesque

Above: *Barcelona's Museum of Contemporary Art is a temple to modernity.*

Barri Xines

The Barri Xines is not a particularly inspiring part of Barcelona, but does have its claim to fame. Serious **Picasso** fans should take a stroll along the **carrer d'Avinyo**, many of the stately houses of which were converted to brothels at the turn of the century. The young Picasso used to spend hours sketching scenes from the street and claims to have had his first sexual experience in one of the brothels. The women from these brothels are said to have inspired the famous *Les Demoiselles d'Avignon* in 1907.

Above: *The fascinating Science Museum has plenty of interactive exhibits.*

cathedral, giving the visitor an idea of the city in former times.
✉ *Plaça del Rei 1, Barri Gòtic,* ☎ *93 315-1111,* 📠 *93 315-0957,* ✆ *museuhistoria@ mail.bcn.es* 💻 *www. museuhistoria.bcn.es* **M** *Jaume I,* 🕐 *10:00– 14:00 and 16:00–20:00 Tue–Sat, 10:00–14:00 Sun; 10:00–20:00 July, Aug and Sep.*

Museu Frederic Marés

This eclectic collection, housed in Palau Reial Major, was donated to the city by sculptor Frederic Marés in 1946. It consists largely of sculptures (pre-Roman to the 19th century), including three floors of crucifixes. The Collector's Room features everything from matchboxes to walking sticks.
✉ *Plaça Sant Iu 5–6, Barri Gòtic,* ☎ *93 310-5800,* ✆ *museomares@ mail.bcn.es* 💻 *www.museomares. bcn.es* **M** *Jaume I,* 🕐 *10:00– 19:00 Tue– Sat, 10:00– 15:00 Sun.*

Museu de la Ciència

A model of a World War II submarine sits in the road outside the museum, and inside there are many buttons to press. For an extra fee, visit the Planetarium, where the night sky is projected onto a dome. Part of the museum is set aside for small children to play with fascinating scientific objects. Parents are not admitted to this haven, but monitors are there to watch the children.
✉ *Teodor Roviralta 55, Sarrià-sant Gervasi,* ☎ *93 212-6050,* ✆ *musciencia.fundacio @lacaixa.es* 💻 *www.lacaixa.es/ fundacio/cat/equips/ museu.htm* **M** *Maria Cristina,* 🕐 *10:00–20:00 Tue–Sun.*

Museu Tèxtil i d'Indumentària

The Textile Museum is housed in an old palace, with a courtyard and an outside stone staircase. It has fabrics from the 4th to the 20th centuries, and accessories such as fans and hair ornaments. There is an exhibition of tools from the Catalan textile industry and a showroom of outfits from famous couturiers including Balenciaga and Pedro Rodríguez.

✉ *Montcada 12–14, Ciutat Vella, Parc,* ☎ *93 310-4516,* ⌨ *museutextil@ mail.bcn.es* 🖥 *www.museutextil.es* **M** *Jaume I,* ⏱ *10:00– 18:00 Tue–Sat, 10:00– 15:00 Sun.*

Museu Arqueològic

This museum offers a good, in-depth study of the background of Catalunya. Exhibits, covering the Costa Brava to the Balearics, span history from the palaeolithic to the Visigothic period. If you plan to visit the Roman remains at Empúries (*see* page 83), it is important to visit this museum first, as it gives a very good background to the Roman site.

✉ *Passeig Santa Madrona 39–41, Sants-Montjuïc,* ☎ *93 423- 2149,* ⌨ *mac@mac.es* 🖥 *www.mac.es* **M** *Poble Sec,* ⏱ *09:30–19:00 Tue– Sat, 10:00–14:30 Sun and public holidays.*

Museu Militar

Old weapons and uniforms evoke images of prisoners taken by Felipe V in the 18th century, and of the Republicans imprisoned in the dungeon during the civil war.

✉ *Castell de Montjuïc,* ☎ *93 329-8613,* **M** *Paral.lel,* ⏱ *09:30– 13:30, 15:30–19:30, Tue–Sun.*

More museums and galleries on pages 14, 15, 18, 26, 32 and 42.)

Joan Miró

Miró's influence is firmly imprinted on Barcelona and can be spotted in the most unlikely places. The ceramic walls at the airport are a Miró design; he also designed the logo for the Spanish Tourist Board and the blue and red starfish of the Caixe de Pensions. Stroll down La Rambla and you'll walk over the huge Miró mosaic on the pavement at Plaça de la Boquería. Also visit the Parc Joan Miró in the northern Eixample to see the famous *Dona i Ocell* (woman and bird) sculpture in the lake.

Below: *A visit to the Archaeological Museum is a worthwhile thing to do before exploring historical Catalunya.*

More Parks
Followers of modern architecture may like to seek out the following:
Parc del Clot: a modern park in the Clot district incorporating a disused railway and old chimney; notable for the sculpture, *The Rites of Spring*, by American Bryan Hunt.
Parc de la Pegaso: a park in La Sagrera on the site of a former factory; it has a sculpture by Ellsworth Kelly.
Parc Joan Miró: a park on the site of an old abattoir, so called because of the artist's famous *Dona i Ocell* statue – a huge, brilliantly coloured model of a woman and a bird.

Below: *Autumn is a good time to enjoy Ciutadella Park.*

Parks and Gardens
Parc d'Atraccions del Tibidabo
Rides in this park include a ferris wheel, roller coaster, children's roundabouts and a rotating vintage aeroplane. A miniature train suspended from a monorail circles the park (see also page 24).
✉ Placa Tibidabo 3, Sarrià-Sant Gervasi, Vallvidrera-les Planes,
☎ 93 211-7942,
🕐 17:00–02:00 Mon–Thu, 17:00–03:00 Fri–Sat, 12:00–23:00 Sun; in winter 12:00–20:00 weekends only.

Parc de Collserola
Wildlife thrives in the city's green lung: red squirrels, wild boar, foxes and the rare genet live under the broom and pine trees.
✉ Ctra Esglesia 92, Sarrià-Sant Gervasi, Vallvidrera-les Planes,
☎ 93 280-3552,
🖥 http://pmpc.amb.es
🕐 09:30–15:00 daily.

Laberint d'Horta
A mansion housing the School of Restoration is set in gardens dotted with statues. Now a public park, the central feature is a magnificent maze of cypress hedges in which it is very easy to get lost. Anyone meeting this fate has to wait to be rescued at sunset, which is when the park keepers come round blowing on their whistles.
✉ Pg Castanyers 1, Horta-Guinardó, Vall d'Hebron,
☎ 93 413-2400.

Other parks and gardens on pages 19 and 23.)

ACTIVITIES
Sport and Recreation

The **Olympic Games** did wonders for the city, with the development of world-class venues for athletics, sailing, track cycling and swimming. There are also facilities for polo, horse riding, ice skating, tennis and squash.

At the **marina** (see page 33 and map A), visitors can take sailing lessons, rent a windsurfer or kayak and even learn scuba diving.

Outside Barcelona, the countryside lends itself to sport. **Cycling** is popular and at weekends country roads are packed with colourful lycra-clad racers. For something a bit more extreme, just 20km (12 miles) from the city is the **Montmeló** Formula One circuit, home of the Grand Prix, where (for a hefty fee) you can learn to drive a Formula One car; 🖳 www.circuitcat.com ☎ 93 571-9777. Visit the Salitre Caves for pot-holing, or Montserrat for off-road driving, abseiling and rope jumping. Other outdoor activities include mountain biking and hot-air ballooning. The foothills of the Pyrenees give opportunities for horse riding, climbing, hiking, paragliding, canoeing, whitewater rafting and, in winter, skiing. Or you could play **golf** on one of the 20 courses in the area – try El Prat, one of the best, about 20km (12 miles) southwest of central Barcelona along the C246; ☎ 93 379-0278.

Football, of course, is a national passion and while visitors are unlikely to play, attending a match at the Camp Nou stadium is a way to sample Barcelona at its most passionate.

Rollerblading

Like most modern cities, Barcelona has a thriving rollerblading culture and on a sunny weekend bladers whizz around the smooth pavements of the new port, the Palau de Mar and the beachfront. When the day trippers have left, the area around the cathedral is a popular haunt at weekends, skaters head for the Parc de la Ciutadella. You can hire roller-blades for a day from the Edelweiss store on Gran Via and even take lessons and tours. For those who prefer to walk, the tourist board produces a guide called *Walks in Barcelona*.

Below: *The Olympic Games in 1992 have inspired city dwellers to keep fit.*

Above: *This sculpture exemplifies the contemporary feel of Barcelona.*

Alternative Barcelona

Barcelona is a liberal and cosmopolitan city with a large **gay population**, much of which moves to the coastal resort of Sitges for weekends during the summer season. There are many bars, clubs and hotels favoured by gays, as well as several events throughout the year, including a gay pride march which takes place on 28 June each year. Additional information can be obtained from **SexTienda**, the gay shop on carrer Rauric in the Barri Gòtic, or **Zeus** on carrer Riera Alta. The weekly listings guide, *Guía del Ocio* (available from newspaper stalls), also features gay clubs and events. Outside the city, however, the conservative country villagers tend to be less tolerant of gay society.

For nightlife with a difference, the **Avinguda del Paral.lel** is the centre of the city's music hall society, with raunchy, Parisian-style shows taking place in theatres like **El Molino**, **Teatre Arnau** and **Teatre Apolo**. More sophisticated variety theatre takes place at the **Belle Epoque**.

Alternatively, ballroom dancing is alive and well, with several grand old venues holding regular classes and sessions in foxtrot, tango and salsa. Try **La Paloma**, **Envelat** and **Bolero**, three of the most fashionable. See the *Guía del Ocio* for details.

Unusual Museums

Barcelona has some bizarre museums: a collection of holograms at **Museu d'Holografia** on Plaça Jaume I, and the Catalan national coin collection at the **Gabinet Numismàtic de Catalunya** in the Palau de la Virreina. Undertakers' cars and carriages are displayed at **Museu de Carrosses Fúnebres** on Sancho de Avila, and the **Museu Tauríon Gran Via** features the heads of famous bulls.

Fun for Children

Spain's biggest adventure theme park (☺ 10:00–20:00 Mar–Nov, but until 24:00 from late June to August), **Port Aventura**, makes a great day out for the whole family. There are plenty of facilities and food stalls in addition to 30 bars and restaurants.

The park is divided into five areas. The **Mediterranean** section doubles as a reception area, with shops selling leather goods and ceramics. The Estació de Nord steam train takes you to the park's other areas.

Dancers in grass skirts and exotic bird displays add a South Pacific feel to the **Polynesian** section. The **Tutuki Splash** is the most popular ride here, hoisting 'boats' up into the heart of a volcano only to send them plummeting into the lagoon below, drenching both passengers and onlookers.

The **Chinese** area contains the park's most famous ride, **Dragon Khan**, a record-breaking roller coaster painted with images of a fiery dragon, that rattles around at speeds of up to 110kph (68mph) and loops the loop eight times.

In the **Mexican** section, a reconstruction of the ancient pyramid of Chichén Itzá is surrounded by jungles, wafting scents of Mexican food and pulsating Mariachi rhythms. The best ride here is **El Diablo**, a runaway train in a silver mine.

The **Wild West** section has a dusty saloon bar and a western stunt show. Rides include the **Grand Canyon Rapids**, 550m (1805ft) of man-made turbulent water, and the **Silver River Flume**, a gentle drift on log-shaped boats.

A Child-friendly City
Barcelona has a lot to offer children, not least two permanent funfairs, one on Montjuïc and one on Tibidabo. There are rides around the city, from the vintage tram at **Tibidabo** to the cable car across the harbour. The Science Museum is a 'hands-on' attraction with lots of buttons to press; the aquarium and **Imax** cinema at the **Maremagnum Centre** (see page 51) are ideal for a rainy day. Kids enjoy the labyrinth at **Horta** and the football museum at **Camp Nou**. For an introduction to arts and crafts, try the **Poble Espanyol** on Montjuïc. The biggest treat, however, is a day at **Port Aventura**.

Below: *Enjoying one of the exciting rides at Port Aventura.*

Below: *The elegant
Plaça Reial is a pop-
ular meeting place.*

Walking Tours
Walking La Rambla
The best time to walk La Rambla is at the
weekend, when most of Barcelona turns out
for a stroll, or on balmy summer evenings as
people perform their nightly *passeig* before
settling outside a bar for tapas and a beer.

Plaça de Catalunya is the geographical
centre of the city, between the Barri Gòtic
(Gothic quarter) and the Eixample. Lawns
and fountains adorn the square, often
packed with people. The Café Zurich on the
corner is popular for morning coffee and
people-watching, though a vantage point
on the terrace carries a premium for drinks.

Walk south from the Plaça de Catalunya
along the **Rambla de Canaletes**, which is
named after an old drinking fountain. Drink
from here, the legend says, and you will
always return to Barcelona. Bookstalls and
news stands line the street, and sundry polit-
ical groups set up tables here, draped with
banners and slogans. When there's a big
football match on, the atmosphere is electric.

Keep walking south. The incessant chirp-
ing of caged birds makes it obvious why the
Rambla dels Estudis is nicknamed '**Rambla
dels Ocells**' (of the birds). A menagerie of
creatures is on sale at the street stalls here:

hamsters, rabbits, macaws,
cockatoos, budgerigars,
even tortoises and fish. On
your right-hand side is the
Església de Betlem (a former Jesuit church), and
opposite is the 18th-
century **Palau Moja**. In
1714, Barcelona's first university stood here.

At the end of this section of the promenade is the entrance to the Mercat Sant Josep, or **La Boquería** (see page 27), after which you will reach the **Rambla dels Flors** (see page 16). Look out for **Casa Bruno Quadros**, designed by Josep Vilaseca – it is adorned with a large, green dragon over the doorway, under which an open umbrella is jauntily hung.

Above: *Rain or shine, buskers and performers entertain the crowds on La Rambla.*

East of Rambla dels Flors is the **Plaça del Pi** (see page 16), with some fascinating buildings. **Casa Josep Roca** is the city's oldest hardware store, with gleaming cutlery displays in its window. The *farmácia*, with its elaborate black and gold window, is typical of turn-of-the-century *modernista* design.

Pavement cafés and restaurants line the **Rambla dels Caputxins**. The most important feature of this section is **Gran Teatre del Liceu**, rebuilt in the late 1990s for the fourth time. Facing it is the **Café de l'Opera**, a city landmark, busy day and night.

In its final stretch, the **Rambla de Santa Monica** widens out onto the seafront. A craft market is usually in evidence here, selling souvenirs and costume jewellery. In this area are the 17th-century **Convent of Santa Monica**, now holding temporary art exhibitions, and the **Palau March** opposite, a neoclassical building from the late 18th century. At the bottom of the street, on the left, is the **Museu de Cera**, or wax museum, with wax figures from the worlds of politics and entertainment; ☉ 10:00–14:00 and 16:00–20:00 Mon–Fri, 10:00–20:00 Sat–Sun. The walk ends at the **Columbus Monument** (see page 33).

Walking La Rambla
Location: Map C
Distance: approximately 1.3km (0.8 miles)
Duration: allow half a day for this walk
Start: Plaça de Catalunya
Finish: Columbus Monument
Route: Heading to the south from Plaça de Catalunya, the five sections of the route are the Rambla de Canaletes, followed by Rambla dels Estudis, Rambla dels Flors, Rambla dels Caputxins and finally the Rambla de Santa Monica.
🍽 Café Zurich, Plaça de Catalunya; Café de l'Opera, Rambla del Caputxins.

Above: *Stunning Casa Ametller was built for a chocolate manufacturer.*

Architectural Walking Tour
Location: Map D–A5, A6, B5
Distance: approximately 1.4km (0.9 miles)
Duration: 2 hours
Start: Passeig de Gràcia metro station
Finish: La Pedrera
Route: South of the Passeig de Gràcia metro station to Mansana de la Discòrdia, then left into carrer d'Aragó as far as Casa Montaner i Simon; go back along carrer d'Aragó, turn left into Passeig de Gràcia, then right into carrer de Mallorca, left into carrer del Bruc, left into Avinguda Diagonal, left into carre de Roger de Llúria, and right into carrer de Provença.

Architectural Walking Tour

Walk south of Eixample's Passeig de Gràcia metro station (take the Passeig de Gràcia exit), and you'll see the **Mansana de la Discòrdia** (Block of Discord) on your right. This trio of extraordinary buildings is so named because of the striking differences in their architectural styles. The first house, **Casa Lleó Morera** at no. 35, was built by Domènech i Montaner in 1905. Probably the least ornate of the three, it is distinctive for its semicircular balconies as well as its colourful entrance of inlaid wood and intricate fruit and flower mosaics. It is not open to the public, but the tiny **Perfume Museum** next door is. Hundreds of bottles line its shelves, ranging from miniature pearl-frosted Roman ampoules to ornate Chinese pots. Designs from the great perfume houses through the ages are also on display; ☺ 10:30–13:00 and 17:00–19:30 daily. Entrance is free.

Casa Ametller, at Passeig de Gràcia 41, was built by Puig i Cadafalch in 1898. The architect experimented with various styles: a Flemish, stepped gable, apricot-and-cream frescoes on the façade, wrought-iron balconies, and *Mudéjar*-inspired tiling in the lobby. Inside is an Art Nouveau stained-glass ceiling. The lights are amazing – dragons rear out from brass fittings under stained-glass shades. Many of the furnishings are by the same architect and can be seen by paying a visit to the **Institut Ametller d'Art Hispanic** on the first floor; ☺ 10:00–13:30 Mon–Fri, 15:30–19:00 Tue–Thu. The third building of the trio is the **Casa Batlló** (*see* page 20).

From here, turn left into the carrer d'Aragó, to find the **Casa Montaner i Simon** on the right, with a giant tangle of wire on the roof. An early *modernista* work by Domènech i Montaner, it houses the **Fundació Tàpies**, the ideal setting for the avant-garde work of Antoni Tàpies. Upstairs is a private library and at the entrance, a shop; ☺ 11:00–20:00 Tue–Sun.

Walk north up the Passeig de Gràcia then turn right into carrer de Mallorca to see two more Domènech i Montaner buildings. **Palau Montaner** is enlivened by its coppery roof trim and ornate mosaic façade. At no. 291 is **Casa Thomas**, with blue and yellow tiles and a different balcony design on each floor. Visit the furniture showroom, and look out for the vast, solid wooden door and the painted, wood-beamed ceiling. The rest of the building consists of private apartments; ☺ 10:00–14:00 and 16:00–19:00 Mon–Fri, 10:00–14:00 Sat.

Next, turn left onto carrer del Bruc and left again onto Avinguda Diagonal to reach the startling **Casa Terrades**, known as **Casa de les Punxes** for its tall, conical spires. It was designed by Puig in 1903. Further along Diagonal, and also designed by Puig, is **Palau del Baró de Quadras**, with its bizarre roof. The **Music Museum** is here; ☺ 10:00–14:00 Tue–Sun, 17:00–20:00 Wed. Opposite, at no. 442, is **Casa Comalat**, the work of **Salvador Valeri** (1873–1954), a disciple of Gaudí. This building is not open to the public.

At the corner of Passeig de Gràcia and carrer de Provença is **La Pedrera** (see page 21).

For other interesting walking tours, visit 🖥 www.barcelonaturisme.com/turisme/ or ☎ 93 368-9730.

Extend the Walk
If you have time, head further north along Passeig de Gràcia (across Diagonal) to **Casa Fuster** at No. 132 – a later work by Domènech i Montaner, built in 1908. His style had matured by the time he designed this building and it carries typical Domènech traits of columns, floral features and dramatic towers, in this case cleverly designed to fit onto a corner block. Another rewarding detour would be to keep going east on carrer de Mallorca after you've visited Casa Thomas, until you reach Gaudí's **Sagrada Família** (see page 22).

Below: *Casa de les Punxes, or the House of Spikes, looks like something out of a fairytale.*

Below: *La Rambla, Barcelona's tree-lined boulevard, is a focal point of the city.*

Organized Tours

Several organized tours are available in and around Barcelona, from short city tours to specialized tours and also excursions away from the city. There are different language options, and many of the tour guides will change the itinerary to suit visitors.

A **four-hour city tour** takes visitors from the Plaza de España, up Montjuïc mountain via the Poble Espanyol, to the Olympic Stadium and then the Mirador del Alcalde for magnificent views of the city. This tour takes in La Rambla and the Passeig de Gràcia, two Gaudí houses – Casa Batlló and Casa Milá – as well as the splendid Sagrada Família church. Finally there is Barri Gótic, where visitors will be able to view the Roman ruins and the cathedral.

There is also an **eight-hour city tour**. This takes in all the sights of the four-hour tour, but in addition includes a stop for lunch in the Olympic Port, where there are various restaurants. The afternoon part of the tour focuses on architecture, viewing more of Gaudí's *modernista* buildings and ending with the Sagrada Família.

Specialized tours include a **shopping tour**, which is a good option if you want to supplement a half-day city tour. The itinerary includes the Pedralbes Centre. The tour guides will be able

to advise you on the best places to shop for various items, including leather.

For **families** with children, there is a tour to Port Aventura theme park (*see* page 43). If the **nightlife** is what particularly interests you, there is a tour of Barcelona by night which includes a tapas dinner as well as a Flamenco show.

There is a **Gaudí architectural tour** which takes in La Pedrera (Casa Milá), Casa Batlló, Sagrada Família and Park Güell. This is a half-day (four-hour) guided tour and is available in several languages. For more information about the Gaudí tour, visit ⌨ www.gaudiclub.com/ingles/i_tour/tour.htm

Further afield, **excursions** are available to places such as Montserrat, Sitges, the wine country, Andorra, Girona and the Dalí Museum, as well as the Costa Brava (*see* pages 78–83). One Costa Brava tour offers dinner in a medieval castle in Lloret de Mar.

For further information, visit ⌨ www.barcelona.com where you will find details of all these tours and more.

Above: *A view of Montjuïc from the beach.*

Right: *The city's busiest shopping street, the Passeig de Gràcia in Eixample.*

Shops
Barcelona Glòries

With some 200 shops selling a range of products from food to fashion, this is the city's biggest shopping centre. Inside are cafés, restaurants and a cinema complex. ⊠ *Avinguda Diagonal 208, Glòries,* ☎ *93 486-0404,* M *Glòries,* ⊕ *10:00–22:00 Mon–Sat.*

El Corte Inglés

A popular department store and one of the most convenient with its four branches. ⊠ *Plaça de Catalunya 14, La Rambla,* ☎ *93 302-1212;* ⊠ *Avda Diagonal 471–473, Eixample,* ☎ *93 419-2020;* ⊠ *Avda Diagonal 617–619, Eixample,* ☎ *93 419-2828;* ⊠ *Portal de l'Angel 19, Barri Gòtic,* ☎ *93 306-3800;* ⊕ *10:00–21:30 Mon–Fri.*

Groc

Antonio Miró is the designer who has put Barcelona on the fashion map. He opened Groc in 1968 and his ranges are beautiful. ⊠ *Rambla de Catalunya 100, Eixample,* ☎ *93 215-7474,* ⊕ *10:00–14:00 and 16:30–20:00 Mon–Sat (the men's department is closed Mon 10:00–14:00, women's department is closed Sat 16:30–20:00).*

Passeig de Gràcia

Barcelona's most fashionable street, the Passeig de Gràcia is 60m (197ft) wide and 1km (⅔ mile) long, lined with designer shops, banks, insurance companies and expensive city apartments. But less than 200 years ago, Passeig de Gràcia was a dusty country lane, linking the walled Barcelona to the village of Gràcia. Five lanes were constructed in 1827 and by 1861, the street had regular coach traffic. There was even a horse-drawn tram in the street's heyday, before the advent of the motor car.

Vinçón

One of Barcelona's best-known style shops, this huge, ultra-modern design emporium holds regular furniture shows in its gallery, once the studio of the artist Ramón Casas. Everything is expensive, but for browsing, the store is a tourist attraction in itself. There are plenty of souvenirs for sale.
⊠ Passeig de Gràcia 93, Eixample, ☎ 93 215-6050, ⊕ 10:00–14:00 and 16:30–20:30 Mon–Sat.

Bulevard des Antiquaris

Many of the more than 70 antique stalls, open at the owner's whim rather than at regular hours, are almost sure to close on Sundays and during the siesta on weekdays. Various goods can be bought here, including furniture, porcelain, Japanese screens, tin soldiers or doorknobs.
⊠ Passeig de Gràcia 55, Eixample, ☎ 93 215-4499.

E4G

This store sells men's and women's clothing, including Calvin Klein, DNKY, Armani, and Miu-Miu, the second line by Prada. There are branches in the Pedralbes Centre and on Tenor Viñas Street, next to Turò Park (the latter closes for siesta).
⊠ Via Augusta 10, Gràcia, ☎ 93 218-7679, M Diagonal, ⊕ g.comella @globalnet.es ⊕ 10:00–20:30 Mon–Sat.

Maremagnum Centre

Families flock here at weekends to feast on tapas and American ice cream, visit the cinemas and browse around the expensive designer shops. There is also an aquarium with an underwater walk through a Perspex tunnel, sharks circling overhead.
⊠ Moll d'Espanya 5–6, Ciutat Vella, ☎ 93 225-8100, ⌨ www. maremagnum.es ⊕ 11:00–23:00 daily.

Shopping Card

A credit card is a good idea if you're exploring the Passeig de Gràcia, where all the best designer shops are located. Anyone visiting the city for professional reasons will also be supplied with a **Shopping Visitor Card**. This card gives discounts at various shops which carry an identifying sticker in the window, and is valid for the visitor's length of stay. With it comes a list of participating stores.

Best Buys
- Spanish ceramics.
- Art books and posters from the museum shops.
- Design items from Vinçón – a popular interior shop.
- Designer clothes from the Boulevard Rosa mall on Passeig de Gràcia.
- Leather shoes for men and women.
- Torró Catalan almond fudge.
- Quince jelly.
- Catalan honey.
- Spicy sausages to take home (well wrapped) from La Boquería market.
- Cava (Spanish champagne).

Below: *Enthusiastic stamp collectors compare notes at the Sunday market on the Plaça Reial.*

Markets
Stamp and Coin Market
This is the gathering place for collectors who come here to buy coins, stamps and rocks. Even if you're not a collector it's worth coming to savour the atmosphere and then have drinks and tapas at one of the bars in the square.
⊠ *Plaça Reial 1, Barri Gòtic,* ☎ *93 318-9312,* **M** *Liceu,* 🖳 *www.bcn.es* 🕘 *09:00–14:30 Sun.*

Els Encants
Also known as Mercat de Bellcaire, this is an authentic flea market selling anything from toys to furniture, clothes and junk. It is crowded on Saturdays, so watch out for pickpockets. Early morning is the best time to go.
⊠ *Plaça de la Glories, Eixample,* ☎ *93 246-3030,* **M** *Glòries,* 🕘 *08:30–18:00 Mon, Wed, Fri, Sat.*

La Boquería (Mercat de Sant Josep)
The city's most comprehensive market, La Boquería (see page 27) sells fruit, vegetables, fresh herbs, cheese, meat, chicken, fish and seafood. There are specialized stalls selling over 40 varieties of olives. Stalls at the entrance are generally more expensive than those further inside.
⊠ *La Rambla 91,* ☎ *93 318-2584,* **M** *Liceu,* 🕘 *08:00–20:30 Mon–Sat.*

Antique Market
On offer here are toys, wooden furniture, jewellery, clothes, books and much more.
⊠ *Plaça de la Catedral, Barri Gòtic,* ☎ *93 291-6100 or 291-6189,* **M** *Jaume I,* 🕘 *10:00–22:00 Thu, Jan–Nov.*

Mercat del Ninot

A traditional market with 175 stalls inside (including grocers, butchers, fishmongers), plus 90 external stalls selling household goods, clothes and gifts. The large central fish stall is impressive, and everything is of high quality.

✉ *Mallorca 133, Eixample,* ☎ *93 453-6512,* Ⓜ *Hospital Clínic,* ⏱ *07:30–14:30 and 17:30–20:30 Tue–Fri, 07:30–15:00 Sat.*

Mercat de la Concepció

This market, revamped in 1998, now has customer parking and shopping trolleys. All the shops provide a home-delivery service. There are various stalls: fruiterers, dairy, butchers, fishmongers and florists.

✉ *Aragón 317, Eixample,* ☎ *93 457-5329,* Ⓜ *Gironal Passeig de Gracial Diagonal,* ⏱ *08:00–20:30 Tue–Fri, 08:00–15:00 Mon, and 08:00–14:00 Sat.*

Mercat de Sant Antoni

This famous market is very big and occupies a whole block. In the centre are the stalls selling fresh fish. Moving outward there are a series of hallways where you'll be able to find fresh fruit and vegetables, meat, chicken, nuts, and much more. It is a bustling market inside, and on Sundays the streets around it also fill up with more stalls selling used books and magazines.

✉ *Comte d'Urgell 1, Poble Sec & Sant Antoni,* ☎ *93 423-4287,* Ⓜ *Sant Antoni,* ⏱ *08:00–14:30 and 17:00–19:30 Mon–Fri, 08:00–14:30 Sat.*

Above: *La Rambla is always buzzing with life as locals and tourists stroll in the fresh air.*

Gourmet Shopping

For hungry sightseers, the following are recommended:

Escribà ✉ Rambla 83. Mouthwatering cakes and pastries in an old building with original *modernista* features.

Fargas ✉ Boteria 16. Hand-made truffles and imported coffees.

Foix ✉ Pl. de Sarrià 12. This upmarket confectioner has been producing legendary cakes since 1886.

Gran Colmado ✉ Consell de Cent 318. Designer deli, ideal for cheese, smoked meat and seafood.

La Pasta ✉ Travessera de Gràcia. Gràcia deli featuring every kind of pasta imaginable as well as sauces, cheeses, herbs and spices.

Above: *Hotel Rey Juan Carlos I, on the Avinguda Diagonal, is one of Barcelona's 'gran luxe' hotels.*

Views of Barcelona

You can arrive at Barceloneta in style by cable car, a breath-taking descent from Montjuïc on a wire supported by only two towers spanning the entire waterfront. This is also a good way to see the old fishing port, with nets piled up on the wharf. Other sweeping views of the city are to be had from the top of Tibidabo; the dizzying spires of the Sagrada Família (only for the brave; the lift emerges onto a narrow stone bridge between two spires); the wave bench in the Parc Güell and, if you're lucky enough to stay there, the upper floors of the deluxe Hotel Arts, the futuristic tower over-looking Barceloneta.

WHERE TO STAY

Hotels in Barcelona are rated according to a star system, with five stars the highest rating. 'Gran Luxe' signifies a very luxurious hotel. **Apartment hotels** have the same grading, the only difference being that they have cooking facilities in the rooms. *Hostals* and *pensións* are more basic, graded from one to three stars. **Camp sites** are rated luxury, first, second and third class and are plentiful. Each region is responsible for its own classification, so gradings will vary from region to region. Most hotels in Barcelona belong to the **Barcelona Hotel Association**. Contact them at ☎ 93 301-6240 to obtain a hotel guide. Most of the **budget** accommodation is located around **La Rambla** and in the **Barri Gòtic**. The right-hand side of La Rambla, looking towards the port, is the safest area. Hostals around **Plaça de Catalunya** are more expensive, but the area is quieter and less threatening at night. Hotels around **Passeig de Gràcia** tend to be the most expensive, but are favoured by many business travellers.

Between Barcelona and the French border are several government-run *paradores* – usually in historical buildings or areas of outstanding natural beauty. For information, contact **Paradores de Turismo**, ✉ carrer Requena 3, 28013 Madrid, ☎ 91 559-0069, 📠 91 559-3233, 🖥 www.parador.es

There are two *paradores* 1–2 hours from Barcelona. **Parador de Cardona** (☎ 93 869-1275, 📠 93 869-1636, ✆ cardona@parador.es) is located in a medieval castle, while **Parador de Vic-Sau** (☎ 93 812-2323, 📠 93 812-2368, ✆ vic@parador.es) overlooks the Sau reservoir and has the tranquil atmosphere of a traditional Catalan farmhouse.

Barri Gòtic and Seafront

• LUXURY

Hotel Arts Barcelona
(Map E–C5)
A five-star overlooking Olympic Marina, a 25-minute walk from La Rambla; managed by Ritz Carlton group. The rooms have fabulous views of the city.
✉ carrer de la Marina 19–21, 08005 Barcelona, ☎ 93 221-1000, ℡ 93 221-3045 (sales), ℡ 93 221-1070 (guests), ✆ rc.barcelona.reservations.manager@ritzcarlton.com ▭ www.ritzcarlton.com

Hotel Colón
(Map E–A3)
Large, traditional hotel facing the façade of the cathedral – in the heart of the Gothic quarter.
✉ Avenida de la Catedral 7, 08002 Barcelona, ☎ 93 301-1404, ℡ 93 317-2915, ✆ info@hotelcolon.es ▭ www.hotelcolon.es

Duques De Bergara
(Map C–B1)
Small, stylish hotel in the Gothic quarter.
✉ calle Bergara 11, 08002 Barcelona, ☎ 93 301-5151, ℡ 93 317-3442, ▭ www.hotelbook.com

Le Meridien Barcelona (Map C–B3)
Recommended for its central location. There is a piano bar with live music, and a fine Mediterranean restaurant.
✉ La Rambla 111, 08002 Barcelona, ☎ 93 318-6200, ℡ 93 301-7776, ▭ www.meridienbarcelona.com

Regente (Map D–A5)
Modernista-style hotel well suited for nightlife; has a rooftop pool and terrace, as well as a good restaurant.
✉ Rambla de Catalunya 76, 08008 Barcelona, ☎ 93 487-5989, ℡ 93 487-3227, ▭ www.ehi.com

Rívoli Ramblas
(Map C–B3)
Four-star, modern design in central location, near Barcelona's best shopping streets.
✉ La Rambla 128, 08002 Barcelona, ☎ 93 302-6643 or 412-0988, ℡ 93 317-5053.

Royal Hotel
(Map C–B3)
Centrally located four-star hotel, with a bar, pizzeria and elegant restaurant serving international and Catalan cuisine.
✉ Ramblas 117–119, 08002 Barcelona, ☎ 93 301-9400, ℡ 93 317-3179, ▭ www.spain-hotels.net/barcelona-hotels/royal/hotel.htm

• MID-RANGE
España (Map C–A4)
Two-star, modernista-style building, with an unusual restaurant design, decorated with elaborate woodwork.
✉ carrer Sant Pau 9, 08001 Barcelona, ☎ 93 318-1758, ℡ 93 317-1134, ✆ hotelespanya@tresnet.com

Gaudí Hotel
(Map C–A5)
This three-star is close to several of the city's cultural attractions.

✉ *Nou de la Rambla St 12, 08001 Barcelona,*
☎ *93 317-9032,*
📠 *93 412-2636,*
✆ *gaudi@hotelgaudi.es*

Gótico (Map B–C3)
This old-style hotel is very well located for sightseeing.
✉ *carrer Jaume I 14, 08002 Barcelona,*
☎ *93 315-2211,*
📠 *93 310-4081.*

Hesperia Metropol (Map B–B5)
Located in the heart of Barcelona, this three-star offers all the comforts of a modern and welcoming hotel.
✉ *Ample 31, 08002 Barcelona,*
☎ *93 310-5100,*
📠 *93 319-1276.*

Hostal Layetana (Map B–C2)
Modest *hostal* next to Roman wall. The service here is friendly and most of the rooms have bathrooms.
✉ *Plaça Ramón Berenguer el Gran 2, 08002 Barcelona,*
☎ *93 319-2012.*

Oriente (Map C–A5)
Central, with reasonable rates. The decor is smart and there is a good restaurant.
✉ *La Rambla 45–47,*
☎ *93 302-2558,*
📠 *93 412-3819.*

Regencia Colón (Map E–A3)
Modern, comfortable hotel in the Gothic quarter. All rooms have a bath, air conditioning, TV and a minibar.
✉ *carrer Sagristans 13–17, 08002 Barcelona,*
☎ *93 318-9858,* 📠 *93 317-2822,* ✆ *info@ hotelregenciacolon.com*

Hotel Rialto (Map C–C5)
This three-star is situated in the Gothic quarter. Rooms with air conditioning, bathroom, individual safe and minibar. There is a good restaurant too.
✉ *carrer Fernando 42, 08002 Barcelona,*
☎ *93 318-5212,*
📠 *93 318-5312,*
✆ *info@hotel-rialto.com* 🖥 *www. hotel-rialto.com*

Suizo (Map B–C3)
Completely modernized and redecorated hotel in the centre of the Gothic quarter. Near the Cathedral, La Rambla, the port and the Picasso Museum.
✉ *Plaça de l'Angel 12, 08002 Barcelona,* ☎ *93 310-6108 or 93 315-0461,* 📠 *93 315-0461.*

• **BUDGET**
Las Flores (Map C–B4)
A simple *hostal* in a central location.
✉ *La Rambla 55, 08002 Barcelona,*
☎ *93 317-1634.*

Marina Folch (Map A–C1)
Clean but basic family-run *hostal*. Near beach, with good restaurant.
✉ *carrer Mar 16 pral, 08003 Barcelona,*
☎ *93 310-3709 or 310-5327,* 📠 *93 310-1062.*

Rey Don Jaime (Map B–C3)
All rooms with a bath, some with a balcony.
✉ *carrer Jaume I 11, 08002 Barcelona,*
☎ *93 310-6208,*
📠 *93 310-6208.*

Eixample

• *LUXURY*

Alexandra
(Map D–A5)
Small, smart four-star near Passeig de Gràcia.
✉ carrer Mallorca 251, 08008 Barcelona, ☎ 93 487-0505,
📠 93 467-7166.

Claris (Map D–A5)
Grand five-star in traditional design, with 24-hour room service. Car rental, tour guide and shuttle service available on request.
✉ carrer Pau Claris 150, 08009 Barcelona,
☎ 93 487-6262,
📠 93 215-7970,
✆ claris@slh.com
🖥 www.slh.com/claris

Condes de Barcelona (Map D–A5)
Smart, in prestigious location near shops and *modernista* buildings. Elegant rooms.
✉ Passeig de Gràcia 73–75, 08008 Barcelona, ☎ 93 467-4780, 📠 93 467-4785, ✆ info@hotel-condesdebarcelona.com
🖥 www.hotelcondes-debarcelona.com

Diplomatic Hotel
(Map D–B6)
Centrally located four-star, excellent for both business and leisure travellers. Some rooms are adapted for the disabled, and there are rooms for non-smokers.
✉ Pau Claris 122, 08009 Barcelona,
☎ 93 488-0200,
📠 93 488-1222.

Gran Hotel Catalonia (Map D–A5)
Modern four-star townhouse hotel near shops, well located for cultural attractions. Friendly staff, comfortable rooms equipped with all the amenities, such as satellite TV.
✉ carrer Balmes 142–146, 08008 Barcelona, ☎ 93 415-9090, 📠 93 415-2209.

Gran Hotel Havana
(Map D–B6)
Four-star in an attractive building. Elegant rooms with facilities such as Italian marble bathrooms, air conditioning and heating, minibar and satellite TV. There are also

meeting and banquet facilities at the hotel.
✉ Gran Via de les Corts Catalanes 647, 08010 Barcelona,
☎ 93 412-1115,
📠 93 412-2611.

Majèstic (Map D–A5)
Large, central hotel, conveniently located near Gothic Quarter, Gaudí houses, Picasso Museum and Liceu Opera House. Facilities include a fitness centre, 24-hour room service and satellite TV.
✉ Passeig de Gràcia 70–72, 08007 Barcelona, ☎ 93 488-1717, 📠 93 488-1880.

Ritz (Map D–A6)
Barcelona landmark, very grand and dignified, located just north of La Rambla. Each stylish room is fully equipped, with air conditioning, TV, minibar, modem connection and safety deposit box. The hotel has its own meeting rooms. Dry-cleaning is available. Wheelchair accessible.
✉ Gran Via de la les Corts Catalanes 668,

08010 Barcelona,
☎ *93 318-5200,*
🖅 *93 318-0148.*

St Moritz (Map D–A6)
This central four-star hotel is in the city's main commercial and tourist area. There is a restaurant and a bar, and rooms have air conditioning, cable TV and a safe.
✉ *Diputación 262, 08007 Barcelona,*
☎ *93 412-1500,*
🖅 *93 412-1236.*

• *MID-RANGE*
Europark (Map E–B1)
This three-star hotel offers soundproof rooms with air conditioning, minibar, TV and safety deposit box. Room service, business facilities and parking are available.
✉ *Aragó 325, 08009 Barcelona,* ☎ *93 457-9205,* 🖅 *93 458-9961,* ⏰ *reservas@ hoteleuropark.com*

Gran Via (Map D–A6)
A three-star hotel housed in an elegant old building. The modern rooms offer

facilities such as air conditioning, en-suite bathrooms, minibar and satellite TV. The hotel also has a large rooftop terrace with a play area for children.
✉ *Gran Via de las Corts Catalanes 642, 08007 Barcelona,*
☎ *93 318-1900,*
🖅 *93 318-9997.*

Podium (Map E–B2)
This recently built hotel has 140 rooms and five suites, as well as business facilities, a fitness centre, a bar and a restaurant. Child care is available, as are valet parking and a laundry service.
✉ *Bailén 4–6, 08010 Barcelona,*
☎ *93 265-0202,*
🖅 *93 265-0506.*

• *BUDGET*
Montserrat
(Map D–A4)
This hotel is very good value for money, considering its prestigious location close to the Gaudí buildings.
✉ *Passeig de Gràcia 114, 08008 Barcelona,*
☎ *93 217-2700.*

Gràcia
• *MID-RANGE*
Minotel Via Augusta (Map D–A3)
Stylish hotel in peaceful location, with air-conditioned rooms. Parking on premises and first-class facilities.
✉ *Via Augusta 63, 08006 Barcelona,*
☎ *93 217-9250,*
🖅 *93 237-7714.*

Montjuïc
• *LUXURY*
Barcelona Plaza Hotel (Map H–B1)
Large four-star with fully equipped communications centre and rooms for conventions. Air-conditioned rooms have TV, minibar and safety deposit box. Modem connections are available. Has a sauna and pools. Wheelchair accessible.
✉ *Plaça España 6–8, 08014 Barcelona,*
☎ *93 426-2600,*
🖅 *93 426-0400.*

Fira Palace
(Map H–B1)
Modern four-star on Montjuïc, ideally located for trade fairs.

All the rooms have air conditioning and full marble bathrooms. The hotel has two restaurants and a bar/lounge and is just minutes away from fine dining, shopping and entertainment. ⊠ Avinguda Rius i Taulet 1–3, 08004 Barcelona, ☎ 93 426-2223, 📠 93 425-5047.

Diagonal

• LUXURY
Avenida Victoria
(Map G–C2)
A comfortable, renovated four-star, in a quiet area near the shops. It has a fine terrace overlooking the pool and gardens. ⊠ Avenida Pedralbes 16, 08034 Barcelona, ☎ 93 280-1515.

Princesa Sofía Inter-Continental
(Map G–B2)
Modern hotel on the Diagonal with excellent convention and business facilities. Refurbished in 1998/99, it has a 24-hour front desk and express check-out service. Car rental is available, also a covered garage and valet parking. ⊠ Plaza Pio X11, 4, 08028 Barcelona, ☎ 93 508-1000, 📠 93 508-1001, ⌨ barcelona@ interconti.com 🖳 www. interconti.com

Barcelona Hilton
(Map G–C3)
Big, modern five-star with all the usual Hilton facilities, such as 24-hour room service, air conditioning, gym, business centre, shops, handicapped access and non-smoker rooms. Situated in the business, commercial and shopping district, it is often busy with convention delegates. ⊠ Avinguda Diagonal 589–591, 08014 Barcelona, ☎ 93 495-7777, 📠 93 405-2573.

Rey Juan Carlos I
(Map G–A2)
Deluxe five-star hotel operated by Conrad Hotels, in beautiful gardens with sporting facilities. (It's a bit too far out of town to walk – use the metro or a taxi.) Accommodation ranges from 30m² standard rooms to the 450m² royal suite. Standard rooms have spacious desks with appropiate lighting and modem connection (fax optional). Popular with convention delegates and business travellers. ⊠ Avinguda Diagonal 661–671, 08028 Barcelona, ☎ 93 364-4040, 📠 93 364-4264, ⌨ hotel@hrjuancarlos. com 🖳 www. hrjuancarlos.com

• MID-RANGE
Hotel Rallye
(Map G–B3)
Small three-star with a bar, restaurant and facilities for the disabled. Air-conditioned rooms with bathrooms. ⊠ Travessera de les Corts 150–152, 08028 Barcelona, ☎ 93 339-9050, 📠 93 411-0790, ⌨ nhrallye@ nh-hoteles.es 🖳 www. nh-hoteles.es

Vegetarian Survival

Vegetarianism is not widely appreciated by the meat-eating Catalans, but there are a few things to choose from on the menu. Useful phrases include: *Sóc vegetariàna* or *Non puc menjar carn* (I can't eat meat). There are plenty of pizza restaurants in town, as well as Indian and Chinese, and a handful of vegetarian restaurants, all of which serve vegetarian options. Self Naturista on carrer Santa Ana is popular, with a changing daily menu and lots of salads, while Illa de Gràcia in Gràcia, ✉ carrer Sant Domènech 19, serves pasta, rice, crêpes and salads.

EATING OUT
What to Eat

Catalan food is influenced by a number of cultures from all over the **Mediterranean** and incorporates pasta from Italy, rice from Byzantine times and rich sauces from France. The area's food has two broad bases: wholesome peasant fare consisting of sausage, pork and dripping on the one hand, and, on the other hand, exquisite seafood fresh from the Mediterranean, for example squid, clams, king prawns, crispy fried anchovies and salt cod.

Expect plenty of rich sauces, thick fish stews and mouthwatering **paella** – giant prawns and chicken pieces nesting on a bed of aromatic saffron rice. While paella actually originated in Valencia, Catalunya has adopted the dish as its own, and varieties of paella are available in specialist restaurants.

Most restaurants offer *pa am tomáquet* as a **starter** – slices of crusty bread rubbed with tomatoes and olive oil. Other starters include pulses, meat and fish; **faves la Catalana**, for example, consists of stewed beans with sliced

spicy sausage, while *canelons* is a pasta dish containing meat and a white sauce. **Vegetarians** will do particularly well with starters; worth trying are *espinacs a la Catalana* (spinach with pine nuts and raisins) and *samfiana* (a tasty hotpot of aubergine, peppers, onions and tomatoes).

In **main courses**, fish and chicken are often mixed, for instance as they are in a paella. Try *lagosta amb pollastre* – lobster in a rich sauce with chicken. Squid in its own ink is very popular here, as is *arros negre*, rice that has been cooked with squid ink.

Fish and shellfish can be grilled (*a la plancha*) or steamed (*a la marinera*) and served with sauce on the side – this could be either *allioli*, a kind of mayonnaise with garlic, or *romesco*, which is a spicy tomato sauce that comes from Tarragona.

Meat dishes include *conill*, which is rabbit; you also get *mongetes amb botifarra* (roast pork sausage with beans that have been cooked in pork dripping) and *escudella de pagès* (a tasty vegetable and meat stew).

Vegetables are not taken very seriously in Catalunya, especially as a main course, but some very tasty **salads** are available. *Escalivada* is a simple aubergine, pepper and onion salad, while *esqueixada* is a green salad with olives, tomato and *bacalao* (salt cod) added to it. *Xato* is a very special salad originating from Sitges, south of the city, and includes anchovies, olives and *bacalao*.

Catalan people have something of a sweet tooth, so **dessert** is a prominent feature on

Above: *Barcelona's oldest restaurant, Casa Culleretes, specializes in Catalan dishes.*
Opposite: *Catalan cuisine is known for doing wonderful things with seafood.*

Above: *Wine merchants in Catalunya stock a tremendous variety of wines.*

the menu. Not to be missed is *crema Catalana*, a creamy custard made of eggs, milk and sugar with a wonderfully crunchy caramelized crust. Otherwise, try the *arros amb llet* (rice pudding), *postres de músic* (a kind of fruit cake), or *mel i mató* (curd cheese with honey). Also look out for *xocolateries*, particularly in the Barri Gòtic area – these tiny hole-in-the-wall confectionery shops sell freshly made chocolate truffles as well as almond and nougat delicacies.

Of course, the cuisine from all over Spain is available at restaurants in Barcelona. You could try the fresh mountain trout stuffed with ham from Andalucía; the seafood pies from Galicia, and *chorizo* and *cocido* – sausages and meat with chickpeas from Castile. You can even have partridge in chocolate from Navarra.

Snacks

While most tourist hotels offer their guests buffet **breakfasts**, the locals tend to stick to coffee with croissants or doughnuts (*churros*). Alternatively they have *Torrades*, which are toasted rolls, and some places serve *truita* (cold tortilla) for breakfast.

At **lunchtime**, plenty of the establishments in the city serve excellent sandwiches made in long, crispy baguettes. While the Spanish tradition is for leisurely three-hour lunches, the reality is that most of the office workers in central Barcelona only have the time to grab a quick snack, just like working people in other cities around the world.

Tapas

No visitor to Spain should miss the **tapas**, mini-portions of snacks on display at the bar in many restaurants. Tapas tend to be served with cocktail sticks and could be anything from a plate of cheese to a few slices of salami or chorizo. The term actually means 'lid' in Castilian Spanish and originates from the small dishes of nuts or olives that bartenders would place over a glass during the last century, apparently to keep the flies out.

Simple tapas used to be free of charge but have evolved into such a **bar culture** that almost every place charges for them now. Nevertheless, a few dishes shared with friends is a fun and cost-effective way to eat. Simply point towards what you want – try croquets of fish or chicken, steamed mussels with tomatoes (*mejillones*), sautéed potatoes with chilli sauce (*patatas bravas*), and garlic fried mushrooms (*champinones*). Real tapas specialists may have up to 30 different dishes on display, including a number of Catalan specialities. Look out for *chipirones* (whole baby squid), *pulpo* (octopus), *caracoles* (snails in a spicy sauce), and *habas con jamon* (broad beans with ham). If you'd like a larger portion, simply ask for a *racion*. The idea, though, is to wander from bar to bar trying a few tapas in each.

Typical Tapas

Tapas are usually displayed under a glass case at the bar so you can point out your selection, but it always helps to interpret the menu. Menus are presented in Castilian and Catalan and the following are tapas typical of the area:
Albóndigas: meatballs in sauce.
Anchoas (Catalan *anxoves*): anchovies.
Boquerones: fresh anchovies fried in a light batter, highly recommended.
Caracoles: snails, usually in a spicy sauce.
Chorizo: spicy sausage.
Croqueta: fish or chicken croquets.
Gambas: shrimp.
Mejillones: mussels.
Patatas bravas: sautéed potatoes in a delicious spicy sauce
Tortilla (Catalan *truita*): Spanish omelette.

Xampanyerias

A few bars in the city specialize in *cava*, the sparkling wine produced in the Penedès region outside the metropolitan area. There are, however, different interpretations of a champagne bar. Some have 30 or more varieties lined up behind the bar for tasting while others sell only one, served in unlabelled bottles at rock bottom prices. The Xampanyet in carrer Montcada, close to the Picasso Museum, sells wine that is semi-sweet and rather low grade, but the bar remains popular with the locals. Elsewhere, bars serving still wine will usually serve *cava* by the glass at reasonable prices.

What to Drink

There are quite a number of wine-producing areas just outside Barcelona, and the best known of these is probably **Penedès**, where the Torres family makes the famous Vina Sol, and the Freixenet and Codorniu houses produce award-winning *cava*, or sparkling wine. The *brut* or *brut nature* (dry sparkling wine) produced in this region bears the closest resemblance to French champagne. Red wines are produced mainly around **Tarragona** and **Priorat**, to the south, while more white wines come from Conca de Barberá.

Wine is grown all over Spain and the most famous varieties are probably the *riojas* (light aromatic reds) from the north and also the wines from **Navarra**, mainly rosés and heavier reds. Both wine and *cava* are served by the glass in many of the tapas bars and also in the city's *xampanyerías*, which are bars of varying quality specializing in sparkling wine or *cava*. Be warned, however, that a *xampanyería* could either mean several vintages behind the bar or, in the case of Xampanyet, one of the most famous, just a semi-sweet fizz served from unlabelled litre bottles with replaceable corks!

The **beer** in Barcelona is the same as anywhere else in Spain, the two most popular brands being **San Miguel** and **Estrella**. **Sangría** is traditionally served on feast days; it is a rather lethal concoction of red wine, lemonade, fruit and brandy which slides down all too easily on a hot summer night.

Barcelona has different kinds of bars that specialize in different types of drink. As well as the aforementioned *xampanyería*, there's a *cervecería* serving mainly beer, or a *cocktelería* serving spirits, as its name implies.

Where to Eat

Barcelona has restaurants serving all kinds of **international cuisine** as well as **regional Spanish** and **Catalan dishes**. Tapas bars, *tascas*, *bodegas*, *cervecerias* and *tabernas* are all types of bars that serve food. Tapas bars and *tascas* serve wine, beer, spirits and snacks, usually displayed at the bar. Budget travellers can substitute a few dishes of tapas for an evening meal. A *bodega* specializes in wine, while a *cerveceria* serves beer. *Taberna* is a generic term for a bar or tavern. A *comedor* is a simple dining room, usually attached to a bar, and a *venta* is a similar set-up in the countryside, usually with a small shop as well. A *marisqueria* specializes in seafood and an *asado* in barbecued food. In any restaurant, the *menu del dia* (the set menu) is good value, usually with three courses and wine. Catalan restaurants are the most common, and some of the more expensive blend French cuisine with local specialities. Fast food ranges from Pizza Hut to Burger King, while ethnic specialities include Indian, Chinese, Middle Eastern and Mexican restaurants.

Above: *Visiting* cava *cellars makes an interesting day trip; Sant Sadurní is just half an hour from Barcelona by train.*

Coffee
Good, strong espresso-style coffee is normally drunk in Barcelona, but there are plenty of alternatives. *Cafe con leche* is made with hot milk, while cappuccino is frothy. *Cafe cortado* is espresso with cold milk. Nescafé invariably means a sachet of decaf. Liqueur coffees are often drunk after meals (and occasionally with breakfast). Try the Café Roma on Plaça d'Angel for an almost bewildering choice.

Below: *Paella is a popular Catalan seafood dish.*

Barri Gòtic

• *LUXURY*
Set Portes
This restaurant is a grand Barcelona institution. It is convenient and very well situated right on the edge of La Ribera. It is rather formal and therefore suitable for business lunches, serving wonderful Catalan specialities.
⊠ *Passeig Isabel 11,*
☎ *93 319-2950.*

• *MID-RANGE*
Amaya
Basque cuisine and tasty seafood are the house specialities in this eatery.
⊠ *La Rambla 20–24, Ciutat Vella,*
☎ *93 302-1037.*

Los Caracoles
A Barcelona legend, this charming establishment serves excellent Catalan specialities in a rambling old building in the Barri Gòtic. It is loud, chaotic and jolly, which makes it good for families. The ambience is touristy.
⊠ *Escudellers 14,*
☎ *93 302-3185.*

El Gran Café
This café serves delicious French/ Catalan specialities. Enjoy your meal to the accompaniment of live piano music.
⊠ *Avinyó 9, Ciutat Vella,* ☎ *93 318-7986.*

Hofmann's
This restaurant is closed on Saturdays and Sundays. During the week, however, they serve great seafood and the most marvellously wicked desserts!
⊠ *Argenteria 74–78,*
☎ *93 319-5889.*

El Salon
This is a restaurant with a very stylish, bohemian feel. Fine French and Catalan specialities are on offer here.
⊠ *c/Hostal d'en Sol 6–8,* ☎ *93 315-2159.*

• *BUDGET*
Museu Picasso
This pretty bar/café is located in the

courtyard of the Picasso Museum (*see* page 18). It has the same opening hours as the museum itself.
✉ *Montcada 15, Ciutat Vella,*
☎ *93 268-3021.*

Gràcia and Eixample

• LUXURY
Botafumeiro
An expensive and prestigious seafood restaurant. It is a formal place, not suitable for children.
✉ *Gran de Gràcia 81, Gràcia,*
☎ *93 218-4230.*

• MID-RANGE
El Pescador
As the name suggests, fish is the speciality of this restaurant.
✉ *Mallorca 314, Eixample,*
☎ *93 459-2564.*

Jean Luc Figueras
Enjoy the stylish setting of this eatery, as well as the tasty Catalan dishes.
✉ *Sta. Teresa 10, Gràcia,*
☎ *93 415-2877.*

Gaig
This popular power-lunching venue serves Catalan cuisine.
✉ *Passeig Maragall 402,* ☎ *93 429 1017.*

La Dama
Elegant, prestigious restaurant housed in a *modernista* build-ing. Catalan cuisine.
✉ *Diagonal 423–425,*
☎ *93 202-0322.*

Tragaluz
This establishment has a trendy bar down-stairs and a light-filled restaurant upstairs. Buzzing at lunch and in the evening, it is a very popular venue for business lunches, and serves Catalonian-Mediterranean food.
✉ *Passatje de la Concepcio 5, Diagonal,*
☎ *93 487-0621.*

La Cuina del Trope
Delight in the comfort of good home cook-ing; this restaurant is situated in an old Barcelona house.
✉ *Passeig de Gràcia 83, Eixample.*

La Gran Tasca
This busy restaurant serves excellent tapas at the bar. It has a lively, informal atmosphere and is especially popular among the locals.
✉ *Balmes 129 bis, Eixample.*

Casi Casi
Excellent Andalucian and Catalan cuisine is served in this establishment.
✉ *c/Laforja 8,*
☎ *93 415-8194.*

El Raco d'en Freixa
This restaurant serves sublime modern cuisine that has been prepared in a most creative manner.
✉ *Sant Elias 22,*
☎ *93 209 7559.*

• BUDGET
El Café de Internet
This centrally located cyber café offers not only good food, but also a fair number of computers to play with.
✉ *Gran Via 656, Eixample,*
☎ *93 302-1154.*

Drugstore David Restaurante Pizzeria

This famous Barcelona eatery is open all night long, and serves a variety of tapas as well as pizza. It has an excellent location among the shops in Eixample. It is always busy; no telephone number is available.
✉ Tuset 19–21.

Seafront
• LUXURY
Lungomare Ristorante

This fashionable Italian restaurant is situated in the Olympic Village.
✉ Marina 16-18, Torre Mapfre,
☎ 93 221-0428.

• MID-RANGE
El Rey de la Gamba

Fabulous seafood dishes are served here, and at reasonable prices.
✉ Porto Olimpic,
☎ 93 221-0012.

L'Emperador

This restaurant offers seafood specialities and has a lovely view over the marina.
✉ Edif. Palau del Mar. Moll del Dipòsit, ☎ 93 221-0220.

Goyescas

Enjoy tapas to die for in the city's most stylish hotel.
✉ Hotel Arts, Carrer de la Marina 19,
☎ 93 221-1000.

Llevataps

Seafood specialities in a setting overlooking the marina.
✉ Plaça Pau Vila s/n, Palau de Mar,
☎ 93 221-2433.

La Oficina

Good value seafood restaurant in the old fishing quarter of Barceloneta.
✉ Passeig Juan de Bourbon,
☎ 93 221-4005.

• BUDGET
Can Majó

Fantastic, bargain seafood can be had here, in the heart of old Barceloneta.
✉ Almirall Aixada 23,
☎ 93 221-5096.

Greater Barcelona
• LUXURY
Casa Ramón

Grills and fondue are the specialities here.
✉ Passeig St Joan Bosco 47, Sarrià,
☎ 93 205-7556.

El Asador de Aranda

Catalan specialities on offer in a spectacular old house.
✉ Avinguda Tibidabo 31, St Gervasil,
☎ 93 417-0115.

BARS

Eating in one of the city's many bars is a great way to try several different kinds of tapas and also to save money. Bars range from the very local to the very lively; those around the Eixample district are mostly smart.

Barri Gòtic
Café de l'Òpera

This rather touristy Art Nouveau bar on La Rambla serves expensive tapas. It is a city landmark, but the service is disappointing. It is always busy and therefore a safe place for single women to go to.

✉ La Rambla 74,
☎ 93 302-4180.

Café de Roma

This lively bar with its invigorating liqueur coffees is situated right on the edge of the Barri Gòtic.

✉ Plaça Angel.

Els Quatre Gats

This charming bar is located in the old quarter of the city (see panel, page 9). It is quite a touristy place, but a must for any Picasso fan.

✉ Montsió 3 bis, Ciutat Vella,
☎ 93 302-4140.

Tèxtil Café

A pleasant café inside the textile museum (see page 38); the opening hours of the café are the same as those of the museum.

✉ Museu Tèxtil I d'Indumentária, Montcada 12–14,
☎ 93 268-2598.

Bar de Pi

Pretty bar located in a shady square just off La Rambla, lively day and night.

✉ Plaça Pi.

Bar Ra

Tapas, tex-mex, and Thai food accompanied by music from jazz to rock.

✉ Plaça de la Garduña 7,
☎ 93 301-4163.

El Velòdrome

A trendy two-storey bar, decorated in Art Deco style with leather sofas.

✉ c/Muntaner 213,
☎ 93 430-5198.

Gràcia and Eixample
Qu Qu

Great deli-style snacks served in a lively atmosphere.

✉ Passeig de Gràcia 24, ☎ 93 317-4512.

Le Pedrera de Nit

Enjoy live music and drinks on the roof terrace of Gaudí's famous building (see page 21). It is open

Saturday and Sunday in summer only; don't miss it if you're in town and it is open.

✉ c/Provença 261–5.

Seltz

This is a specialist vermouth bar with excellent tapas.

✉ carrer Rosselló 154,
☎ 93 453-6099.

Tragaluz

Trendy bar with Japanese menu.

✉ Passatje de la Concepcio,
☎ 93 487-0196.

Seafront
Tardá Rock

Barcelona's own rock café, packed with memorabilia. Serves Tex-Mex food.

✉ Marina 16–18 Torre Mapfre, Port Olympic,
☎ 93 221-3993.

Greater Barcelona
Bar Tomás

Bar in the Tibidabo area, attracting a lively crowd.

✉ Mayor de Sarrià 49,
☎ 93 418-8855.

Above: *At night the brightly lit façade of La Seu dominates the lively streets of the Barri Gòtic.*

The Passeig

The *passeig* – an evening walk or stroll – is an essential component of Barcelona nightlife in the summer months. When offices have closed, locals slowly parade the city's trendiest areas, stopping for tapas and to greet friends. A second *passeig* takes place between tapas and dinner, usually around 23:00, after which most people repair to a bar and then a nightclub. The best locations for people-watching are La Rambla, packed with outdoor bars and cafés; on Montjuïc to watch the sunset; Plaça del Pi in the Barri Gòtic; and the Gran Via de les Corts Catalanes. One of the newer areas for outdoor drinking is the Moll de la Fusta, the seafront by the Barri Gòtic, developed for the Olympic Games.

ENTERTAINMENT
Nightlife

Barcelona comes alive after dark and buzzes until dawn. There's a lot to choose from: live jazz, classical music, funfairs, discos, flamenco shows and endless bars (*see* pages 68–69).

Everything happens late in Barcelona. Go for a stroll at sunset, nibble a few tapas and enjoy a drink. Then move on to a restaurant at around 22:00. After dinner, many people go to another bar before going on to a disco or *discoteca* at midnight. Some stay open until 06:00. You need stamina for this city!

In **La Rambla** and **Barri Gòtic**, Plaça del Pi and the Plaça Reial are the most atmospheric places on a summer night with outdoor seating. There are some good bars in the Barri Xines, best visited with a local, and along the Passeig de Born. Try Ample and Mercé, two streets forming the southern border of the Barri Gòtic, for authentic bars where wine is poured from barrels and free tapas are sometimes handed out.

In **Gràcia** and **Eixample**, by far the most fashionable area, a string of designer tapas bars are found along the Passeig de Gràcia. The best discos, often with startling decor and beautiful people, are here and needless to say, the prices match the venues.

Along the **Waterfront**, many good fish restaurants in the old fishing village of Barceloneta have been moved to a trendy warehouse conversion, Palau de Mar, becoming fashionable tapas bars in the process. Further north, the Olympic Marina buzzes with life in summer with over 50 bars and restaurants overlooking the yacht basin.

Also worth a visit is **Montjuïc**, where the bars around the Poble Espanyol get very lively in the summer and there's an exceptionally popular club, Torre de Avila, with moving walls and transparent floors.

Spend a night in **Girona**, a city which deserves more than a day trip. Like Barcelona, it has a Rambla where everybody takes their evening *passeig*. Nightlife revolves around the new part of the city across the river from the old town where there are rows of excellent bars alongside the majestic Parc de la Devesa. In winter, the bars around Plaça Ferran el Católic are more popular. For a quieter scene, there are plenty of places to eat and drink in the old quarter.

Nightlife in **Sitges** (*see* page 79) is fast and furious, mainly in the town centre. The carrer 1er Maig is the heart of the action with a long line of discos, pubs, restaurants and cocktail bars. Some discos are exclusively gay but there's a happy atmosphere in Sitges and holiday-makers mix cheerfully with drag queens, partygoers and artists. Having said this, Sitges is probably not the best choice for the faint-hearted.

Designer Bars

A night out in Eixample is a must, if only to sip one expensive drink per bar. Start at **Seltz**, a high-fashion bar dedicated to vermouth and serving excellent tapas, on Carrer Rosselló. **Tragaluz**, on Passatge de la Concepcio, has a Japanese menu and designer furniture. **Tapa Tapa** at no. 44, Passeig de Gràcia, serves *cava* by the glass while **Dry Martini** on carrer d'Aribau serves every possible form of martini cocktail. At around 01:00, head for **Nick Havana** on carrer del Rosselló, a futuristic nightclub with a cowhide bar by Philippe Starck and a video wall.

Below: *'Designer' tapas are a feature of the non-stop Barcelona nightlife.*

> **Barcelona for Hire**
> Feeling generous? Some of Barcelona's most unique venues can be hired for private parties. You could throw a cocktail party at the top of the Torre de Collserola or take over the Gothic hall at La Llotja, the neoclassical stock exchange, for a banquet. Parties also take place in the Codorniu *cava* cellars in the wine region, the Casa de l'Ardiaca in the Barri Gòtic and the Hivernacle greenhouse in Parc de la Ciutadella. Perhaps the most coveted place of all in which to entertain is Gaudí's Casa Batlló – at a price, naturally.

Below: *Many different ent kinds of music, from jazz to classical, are performed in Barcelona.*

Music

Barcelona has some of the best nightlife in Spain and is a wonderful place in which to enjoy live music, from **jazz** in smoky basement bars to exuberant **Latin American**, where people dance on the tables. Folk music is growing in popularity and its most famous expression today is in the **Sardana**, the national dance of Catalunya, performed on Sunday in front of the cathedral.

An experience to remember is a classical concert in the stunning **Palau de la Música Catalana** in the Gothic quarter, one of Domènech i Montaner's *modernista* masterpieces – all ornate sculpture and stained glass. This concert hall has long been seen as the spiritual home of Catalan music. Also memorable is an opera in the new **Liceu**, which promises to be one of Europe's most spectacular opera houses (*see page 73*); here you may be lucky enough to see a performance by the legendary soprano **Montserrat Caballe**, Catalunya's most famous daughter.

Another concert venue you could try is the **Saló de Tinell** (the place where the Spanish Inquisition once sat), the Gothic hall of the Palau Reial in Barri Gòtic, where free music recitals frequently take place. A variety of exhibitions and other events are also held regularly in this lofty, handsome hall.

Theatre

Barcelona's **Liceu**, once one of Europe's largest opera houses with a capacity of over 5000, has a history riddled with disaster. The pride of the city, the building was founded in 1847. Destroyed by fire in 1861, it was rebuilt and soon became the talk of Europe, attracting a number of legendary figures of Italian and German opera.

In 1893, two bombs were thrown onto the stage during a performance of *William Tell*, killing 20 people. The theatre was repaired again.

Then in January 1994, a worker's blowtorch set fire to some of the scenery, razing the building to the ground. Yet again, the opera house rose from the ashes – today the auditorium has been recreated in red velvet and gold leaf, and the subterranean foyer is used for talks, late-night recitals or puppet shows.

Another striking venue is the **Teatre Nacional de Catalunya**. Designed by architect Ricard Bofill, it resembles the Parthenon and is the most imposing theatre building in the city. The TNC, as it is known, stands alone on a grand lot near the Plaça de les Glòries.

Don't miss the *Grec* season that takes place in July and August every year. This is a summer festival offering a wide variety of outdoor entertainment centred around the open-air **Teatre Grec** (Greek Theatre) on Montjuïc. Open-air theatre or music on a hot summer's night is always a magical experience, and the Teatre Grec couldn't be a more beautiful setting – among scented subtropical gardens, with the city lights glittering far down below.

Open-air Barcelona
Don't miss the **Dia de Sant Joan** festival on 23 June each year, when fireworks are set off all over the city and the atmosphere is festive. Also in June is the **Caixa flamenco festival**, when the Andalucían population parties late into the night.

Gran Teatre del Liceu
✉ La Rambla 51–59
☎ 93 485-9900
📠 93 485-9918
🖥 www.liceubarcelona.com
Ⓜ Liceu
🕐 09:00–14:00 and 16:00–19:00 Mon–Fri
🕐 box office 10:00–13:00 and 15:00–19:00 Mon–Fri

Palau de la Música Catalana
✉ carrer Sant Francesc de Paula 2, Eixample
☎ 93 295-7200
📠 93 295-7210
🖥 www.palaumusica.org
Ⓜ Urquinaona
🕐 box office 10:00–21:00 Mon–Sat, 1 hour before concert Sun (concert days only)

Teatre Nacional de Catalunya
✉ Plaça de les Arts 1, Eixample
☎ 93 306-5700
Ⓜ Glòries
🕐 box office 12:00–15:00 and 16:00–21:00 Mon, 12:00–21:00 Tue–Sat, 12:00– 18:00 Sun.

Festivals

Catalan festivals are exuberant affairs, the streets decked with bunting, red and yellow Catalan flags fluttering, bands playing and people dancing in the streets. Festivals take place for all kinds of reasons – national holidays, saints' days or pagan rituals.

Every village has a saint's day and the celebrations give an insight into Catalan culture. The whole village parades behind an effigy of the saint with much drinking and dancing as the procession winds its way to the countryside for huge picnics and more merrymaking.

Certain sights are unique to Barcelona. On 23 April, **St George's Day**, the patron saint of Catalunya is celebrated with gusto. Everybody dresses as a devil or an animal and parades noisily through the streets, letting off firecrackers. On 24 September is **La Mercé**, the main festival of the city's calendar, when *gegants* (giant papier-mâché figures in brilliant colours) are marched through the city to the **Plaça de Sant Jaume**. At the same time, huge human towers, or *castells*, are built up to 10m (33ft) high, the challenge being for a young boy to climb to the top. The night sky is ablaze with fireworks and live bands play in every square. (For more festivals, *see* panel on this page.)

Casinos

There are three casinos within easy driving distance of Barcelona, although none in the city itself. The first, **Gran Casino de Barcelona** at Sant Pere de Ribes, a town near Sitges on the Costa Daurada, is housed in a mansion and has a nightclub as well as the usual gaming rooms. (You will have to show an ID card, passport or driving licence in order to gain access to the gaming rooms.) On offer are French and American roulette, blackjack, boule, banco and various gaming machines. There is also a restaurant ('The King', serving international haute cuisine) and a cafeteria ('The Queen', with a buffet service). The discotheque, 'Baccara', is open until 04:00.

The **Casino Castell de Peralada**, in the Empordà region, is situated in a 14th-century castle, which also houses a fine library and museum. Proof of identity is required for access to the gaming rooms, and all the usual games can be played here. There is a restaurant, 'Castell de Peralada', as well as function rooms which may be hired for weddings or conventions.

The glitzy **Casino Lloret de Mar**, located in the eponymous holiday resort on the Costa Brava, is more modern. It offers similar services and games as the other two casinos.

For less effort, casual gamblers can try the **Spanish lottery**. Buy a ticket from any *loteria* booth, of which there are plenty throughout the city. The results are published the day after the draw in most newspapers. On 22 December, **El Gordo** (the fat one), the biggest draw of the year takes place and the whole of Spain stops work to listen to the result.

Gran Casino de Barcelona
✉ Marina 19–21, Marina Village
☎ 93 225-7878 or 221 8572
📧 gcb@casinos-catalunya-com
🖥 www.casinos-catalunya.com/gcb
🕐 13:00–05:00 daily

Casino Castell de Peralada
✉ northern Costa Brava, 20 km from France
☎ 97 253-8125 or 253-8087
📧 peralada@casinos-catalunya-com
🖥 www. casinos-catalunya.com/peralada
🕐 gaming room 19:00–04:00 Mon–Thu, 14:00–05:00 Fri, Sat and days before public holidays, 11:00–05:00 Sat, 11:00–04:00 Sun and holidays.

Casino Lloret de Mar
✉ Lloret de Mar (Girona), 80km from Barcelona, Costa Brava
☎ 97 236-6116 or 236-3106
📧 lloret@ casinos-catalunya-com
🖥 www. casinos-catalunya.com/ lloret
🕐 live cabaret takes place at 21:30 on Sat.

Opposite: *Dragons are the central theme of St George's Day, celebrated on 23 April.*

Spectator Sports

Football

Football tickets are available at the stadium a week before a match.

✉ *FC Barcelona Camp Nou, Avda Ar'stides Maillol, Les Corts,* ☎ *93 496-3600,* **M** *Maria Cristina,* 🖳 *www. fcbarcelona.com* 🕘 *ticket office open 09:30–13:30 and 16:30–19:30 Mon–Fri.*

American Football

American football games take place at 17:00 on Saturdays, from April to June.

✉ *Barcelona Dragons, Estadi Ol'mpic de Montjuïc, Avda de l'Estadi 17–19, Montjuïc,* ☎ *93 425-4949,* **M** *Espanya or Paral.lel,* 🖳 *www.dragons.es* 🕘 *the ticket office opens two hours before kick- off on match days.*

Basketball

Basketball is the second most popular sport in Barcelona, coming a close second after football. The season runs from September to May; most of the league games are played on Saturday and Sunday evenings.

✉ *Club Joventut Badalona, carrer Ponent 143–161, Badalona, Outer Limits,* ☎ *93 460-2040,* **M** *Gorg,* 🖳 *www.penya.com* 🕘 *ticket office opens one hour before match times.*

Right: *FC Barcelona is one of Spain's top football teams.*

Nightclubs

Blue Note

This venue offers live jazz performances.

✉ *Caller Aragó 221, Eixample,*

☎ *93 454-6321.*

Dry Martini

Fashionable bar serving every permutation of a dry martini.

✉ *carrer d'Aribau 162, Eixample.*

Garatge Club

Live music and several dance floors.

✉ *carrer de Pallars 195, Sant Martí.*

Oliver & Hardy

Busy *discoteca*, open until 04:00.

✉ *Avinguda Diagonal,*

☎ *93 419-3181.*

KGB

Fashionable warehouse-style club with spying theme.

✉ *carrer Alegre de Dalt 55, Gràcia,*

☎ *93 210-5906.*

Nick Havanna

Trendy designer bar with cowhide-covered bar and huge video wall. Popular with 30-somethings after 01:00.

✉ *carrer del Rosselló 208,* ☎ *93 215-6591*

Universal

Dancing and space for chilling out and conversation.

✉ *Maria Cubi 184,*

☎ *93 201-4658.*

Otto Zutz

The trendiest of all, frequented by supermodels. Warehouse conversion with dancing on three levels. Dress fashionably.

✉ *Lincoln 15,*

☎ *93 238-0722.*

Tablao de Carmen

Flamenco performances in summer; touristy but interesting and atmospheric.

✉ *Arcs 9, Poble Espanyol,*

☎ *93 325-6895.*

Torres de Avilá

Futuristic designer club in the Poble Espanyol.

✉ *Marqués de Comillas s/n, Montjuïc,*

☎ *93 424-9309.*

Night Owls

Commonly known as *discotecas*, Barcelona's nightspots are among the most sophisticated in Spain. Some are bars with dancing, while others are nightclubs only. Some have an entrance charge, others are free before midnight. Some have live entertainment, and a few have a door policy. A bar with music may close at 02:00 or 03:00 while a disco will stay open until 05:00 or even later at weekends. The *Guia del Ocio*, Barcelona's weekly listings guide, will have details of what's on in all the trendiest nightclubs. (Beware of using the term 'club'; it usually implies a sex show and you may be directed to the Barri Xines!)

Above: *Fun-loving Sitges has its peaceful side too, as can be seen in the old town centre.*

Devil's Bridge
At the town of **Martorell**, about 25km (16 miles) northwest of Barcelona, is a highly unusual bridge, the **Pont del Diable**, which crosses the River Llobregat. Popular legend says that the bridge was built by **Hannibal** in 21BC with its central triumphal arch in memory of his father Hamilcar Barca, allegedly the founder of Barcelona. The less romantic reality is that the Romans built the bridge, which was extended in the Middle Ages and is in a remarkable state of repair today.

EXCURSIONS

Beyond Barcelona, a fascinating hinterland waits to be explored. To the south, the golden beaches of the **Costa Daurada** extend to the city of **Tarragona**, the rolling hills and fields inland lined with endless grape vines. An easy trip from the city is to the cellars of **Sant Sadurní d'Anoia**, heart of the sparkling wine producing area, or the town of **Vilafranca del Penedès**, where some of the country's best still whites are produced.

High spot on the Costa Daurada for partygoers is **Sitges**, a flamboyant holiday resort with a colourful community that arrives for the summer. For families, **Port Aventura** (*see* page 43) is a better bet – Spain's biggest, most advanced theme park, where you'll enjoy a day watching street entertainers, riding the roller coasters and sampling food from all over the world.

You really should go inland to visit **Montserrat** (*see* pages 25 and 82), a vast chunk of wind-eroded limestone that has been a shrine for over 1000 years. To the north, the beaches of the **Costa Brava** beckon, a string of sandy bays forming one of Spain's most beautiful coastlines. At the northern end of this coast, the eccentric **Salvador Dalí Museum** (*see* page 26) in Figueres is the main attraction, while inland the lovely medieval city of **Girona** (*see* page 71) and the mountain principality of Andorra merit at least a day each.

Car hire gives you more freedom to follow these itineraries but all are easily accessible by Catalunya's excellent public transport system, using train, bus, cable car or boat.

Sitges

Sitges initially developed as a holiday resort for rich city residents, many of whom still have a second home on the beach. The resort blossomed in the 1960s to become Spain's leading gay centre as well as a weekend hangout for young city people. **Carnival** in February sees the gay community organizing its own agenda of unofficial events, including an exuberant **drag parade** on Mardi Gras Tuesday.

A pleasant fishing village turned holiday resort, Sitges features two big beaches right in the town. Further out are nudist beaches and even gay nudist beaches. The town has a couple of sights, though life in Sitges for most involves commuting slowly between the attractive, open-air coffee bars and the beach.

Overlooking the beaches is an eccentric museum, **Cau Ferrat**, former home of the artist Santiago Rusiñol (1861–1931). It contains a jumble of Rusiñol's work and various purchases and gifts, including paintings by **El Greco** and **Picasso**.

Next door in the **Palau Maricel de Mar** is a small, mixed collection of Romanesque and Gothic paintings, an attractive collection of Spanish ceramics, and wall paintings by the artist Josep Maria Sert (1874–1945). One more museum in the old part of the town, the **Museu Romàntic**, displays everyday items from the life of a wealthy family in the 18th and 19th centuries, including music boxes and puppets.

For information on nightlife in Sitges, *see* page 71.

For information on nightlife in Sitges, *see* page 71.

Sitges
Location: Map J–B2
Distance from city:
29km (18 miles)
🕐 09:30–14:00 and 16:00–18:00 Tue–Sat, 09:30–14:00 Sun
(Cau Ferrat)
🕐 09:30–14:00 and 16:00–18:00 Tue–Sat, 09:30–14:00 Sun
(Palau Maricel de Mar and Museu Romàntic)

Below: *Bronzed bodies pack the beach at Sitges.*

Wine Country
Location: Map J–B2
Distance from city:
Sant Sadurní is half an
hour from Barcelona by
train. Vilafranca is easily
accessible by train or a
short drive, making this
an ideal half-day trip.
🚌 Use public trans-
port from Barcelona or
else hire a car.
🕐 10:00–14:00 and
16:00–19:00 Tue–Sun
(Wine Museum in
Vilafranca)

Wine Country

South of Barcelona are the vineyards, which
produce 100 million bottles a year of *cava*,
the Spanish version of *methodé champ-
enoise*. The town of **Sant Sadurní** has been the
heart of the *cava*-producing region for over
a century. The first wine grower to try the
Champagne method was **Josep Raventós i
Domènech**, copying the techniques of Dom
Perignon in 1872. His family still produces one
of the best labels today, **Codorníu** – tours of the
cellar can be arranged. The ivy-draped Codorníu
building, designed by Puig i Cadafalch, blends
in well with the vineyards around the town.

The other big producer here is **Freixenet**,
with its cellars opposite the train station. Tours
and tastings can be arranged here as well.

Vilafranca del Penedès is the capital of
the region's wine industry and has been a
bustling market town since the 11th century.
The wines from this area are almost all white,
made from three types of grape: **Macabeu**,
Xarel.lo and **Parellada**. Wine *bodegas* (cellars)
are dotted all over town and most arrange
tours and tastings. One of the biggest pro-
ducers here is **Torres**, a flagship for the whole
of Spain, whose dry, fruity Vina Sol is exported
worldwide. Good wines to try are Gran Vina
Sol, flowery Esmeralda, Gran Coronas and Los
Torres Merlot.

Below: *The area
around Sant Sadurní
is well known for its
sparkling wines.*

The **Wine Museum** is
worth a visit. Located in
a 12th-century palace
that was once home of
the Kings of Aragón, it
tells the story of wine
production and drinking
from Roman times up to
the 15th century.

Tarragona

An hour or so along the highway southwest of Vilafranca del Penedès is the town of Tarragona, former capital of the Roman province and a paradise for keen hunters of **Roman remains**.

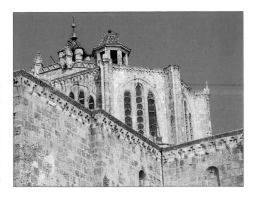

Above: *The walls of Tarragona's cathedral display intricate stonework.*

Visit the old town on foot by following the Passeig Arqueològic, a pathway between the city's Roman walls and the much newer outer fortifications, built in 1707. Every so often there's a *mirador* (lookout point) either over the plains or the sea, and historic paraphernalia is displayed along the route including Roman columns and 1000-year-old cannons.

Within the walls of the medieval part of town is the **cathedral**, a mixture of Gothic and Romanesque styles, and two fascinating **museums** covering the city's history and archaeological treasures. Beneath the town, on the grassy slopes leading down to the sea is a magnificent **Roman amphitheatre**, while along the Rambla Valla are the remains of the Roman circus, **Circ Romà**, where chariot racing took place.

The most spectacular remains, however, are at the **Museu i Necropolis Paleocristians**. Excavations of this vast burial site have revealed pagan and Christian tombs dating back to the 3rd century AD, the riches of which are displayed in the museum. Look for urns, tombs, sarcophagi and Visigothic sculpture.

If travelling in the area with children, be sure to visit **Port Aventura** (*see* page 43).

> **Tarragona**
> **Location:** Map J–A2
> **Distance from city:** 83km (52 miles)
> ☻ 10:00–20:00 Tue–Sat, 10:00–15:00 Sun Apr–Sep; 10:00–17:30 Tue–Sat during winter (Roman ruins)
> ☻ 10:00–13:00 and 16:30–20:00 Tue–Sat, 10:00–14:00 Sun (Museu i Necropolis Paleocristians)

Above: *Hundreds of flickering candles light the grotto at Montserrat.*

Montserrat

A highlight of the Barcelona area (*see* page 25), Montserrat makes a wonderful excursion. Montserrat is important to Catalans because it is a symbol of the region's revival. When the **abbey** was restored in the mid 19th century it marked the beginning of Catalunya's cultural renaissance. There are now some 80 monks living here, as well as 50 students at the world-famous **choir school** (Escolania).

The visit begins with a breathtaking ascent by cable car to just below the monastery, or a drive up the zigzagging mountain road. Outside the monastery, a small city has sprung up to accommodate thousands of tourists – there is a restaurant, several souvenir shops, an information centre and even a bakery. In the monastery, only the 16th-century **basilica** is open to the public.

A second cable car descends to **Santa Cova**, the holy grotto, where the original Virgin icon is said to have been left by St Peter. A tiny chapel was built here in the 17th century, containing a replica of the statue.

A third cable car heads up to Sant Joan, with a short trail to a mountain restaurant. Hikers may spend a night on the mountain at one of two tiny refuges; obtain permission from the **FEEC** (*Federació d'Entitats Excursionistes de Catalunya*) in Barcelona.

The **Museu de Montserrat** has two sections. The old part includes architectural remains from the hermitages on the mountain and some excellent work by El Greco and Caravaggio, while the new area features mainly 19th-century Catalan art.

Costa Brava

The Costa Brava, a mix of quiet coves and brash resorts, stretches from Barcelona to the French border. **Lloret de Mar** is where thousands of pale north Europeans toast themselves by day and party at night. Fragments of an old town remain around the Plaça de l'Església but hedonism rather than history is the essential flavour here. In contrast, **Tossa de Mar**, 12km (7½ miles) north, is a walled tangle of streets and 12th-century buildings on a rocky headland. The town was originally Roman and the old town, the **Vila Vella**, is delightful. The **Museu de la Vila Vella** has some Chagall paintings on display.

North of Tossa de Mar, the coast road is a series of perilous hairpin bends with constant flashes of deep blue sea. **Sant Feliu de Guixols** is actually over 1000 years old, despite the inevitable bars and cafés that have sprung up. Founded in 1277, **Palamós** is a busy fishing town around a picturesque harbour. The 16th-century market town of **Palafrugell** has virtually escaped the ravages of development.

Empúries is best known for its Roman remains. The 40ha (99-acre) site is still being excavated and is a fascinating place to wander around. There is a museum, the **Museu d'Arqueologia de Catalunya**, by the Roman cisterns. Some of the more valuable finds, however, are housed in the **Archaeological Museum** on Montjuïc in Barcelona (see page 39). Visit the Barcelona museum first for valuable background information.

> **Costa Brava**
> **Location:** Map J–E2, J–F2
> **Distance from city:** Lloret de Mar is about 67km (42 miles) from Barcelona
> ☎ 97 277-0208 (museum in Empúries)
> 📠 97 277-4260 (museum in Empúries)
> 🕐 10.00–13:00 and 15:00–18:00 Mon–Sat, 10:00–13:00 Sun (Museu de la Vila Vella)
> 🕐 10:00–14:00 and 15:00–20:00 Tue–Sun (museum in Empúries)

Below: *Tiny, hidden coves line the coast of the Costa Brava.*

Above: *The Passeig de Gràcia was originally a horse and carriage track to the village of Gràcia.*

Disabled Access
The staging of the Paralympic Games in Barcelona in 1992 did a lot to improve disabled access within the city and new buildings, by law, must now be fully accessible. The Barcelona museum guide has full details of museum accessibility and the Spanish Tourist Board produces a fact sheet of useful contacts and places to stay, though public transport, notably buses and trains, is inconvenient for wheelchair users. **ONCE**, the organization for the blind, ⊠ carrer Calabria 66–76, publishes a braille map of the city.

Best Times to Visit

Spring and **autumn** are probably the best times to visit, as the weather is mild, making conditions ideal for exploring the city on foot. **Winter**, however, also has its advantages in that there are no queues to wait in. Some of the attractions will be closed in the winter months – these include the Montjuïc cable cars and the amusement parks. Outdoor venues such as the **Poble Espanyol** and the **Olympic Marina** are also rather deserted and the coastal resorts are very quiet. **High summer** is usually too hot to pound the streets, although the evenings are pleasantly warm. Some restaurants shut down during August, which is when Spaniards generally take their annual holiday, and the coastal resorts, not surprisingly, are packed at this time.

Tourist Information

The **Spanish Tourist Board** has offices in the United Kingdom (London); the USA (Chicago, Los Angeles, Miami and New York); Canada (Toronto); Australia (Sydney) and most European countries;
🖳 www.tourspain.es
Useful websites are:
🖳 www.barcelona.com and 🖳 www.barcelona-on-line.es
The Barcelona Town Hall website, packed with information, is:
🖳 www.bcn.es
The excellent **Barcelona tourist board** has offices around the city:
Estació Barcelona Sants, ⊠ Plaça Països Catalans, s/n, station vestibule;
🕘 open 08:00–20:00 Monday–Friday, 08:00–14:00 Saturday, Sunday and public holidays; 🕘 open 08:00–20:00 daily in summer. Information about Barcelona only. The Barcelona tourist board also has a very active **Convention Bureau** for assistance

with event planning and trade fairs.

Tourist Information Office: ✉ Gran Via de Les Corts Catalanes 50, ☎ 93 301-7443, ⊕ open 09:00–19:00 Monday–Friday, 09:00–14:00 Saturday. Closed Sundays and public holidays.

Barcelona Airport, International Terminal, ☎ 93 478-4704; ⊕ open 09:30–20:30 Monday–Saturday, 09:30–15:00 Sundays and public holidays. Tourist information on Barcelona, Catalonia and the rest of Spain.

Entry Requirements

All visitors need a **passport** or in certain cases, an **identity card**. Citizens of Andorra, Liechtenstein, Monaco, Switzerland and countries within the EC need only present an identity card, with the exception of Denmark and the UK, citizens of which need a passport. UK visitors must have a full ten-year passport as of 1995. Japanese, Canadian and US citizens require a passport but no visa. Citizens of Australia and New Zealand require **visas**. All visitors can stay up to 90 days, after which time a **residence permit** is required.

Customs

The maximum allowance for duty-free items brought into Spain is as follows: one litre of spirits or two of fortified wine; two litres of wine and 200 cigarettes. When the items are bought and duty paid for in the EC, the amounts are 10 litres of spirits, 90 litres of wine and 110 litres of beer, for private consumption only. There is not much point bringing wine or beer into Spain, as they are cheap locally. You can no longer buy duty-free goods if you are travelling within the EC. **Andorra** is entirely duty free and is a good place to buy cheap alcoholic drinks, cigarettes and perfume. Euro and foreign currency, banker's drafts and traveller's cheques can be imported and exported without being declared, although an upper limit applies. Spanish custom officials are generally polite and easy to negotiate with.

Health Requirements

No vaccinations are required to enter Spain and the only health hazards are the occasional upset stomach and the sun, which is very strong in summer (June to September). EU citizens qualify for free medical treatment on presentation of the appropriate form (the **E111** for British citizens). Visitors from elsewhere should arrange their own travel and medical insurance.

Getting There

Barcelona is accessible by road, rail, air and sea with domestic connections vastly improved since the Olympic Games in 1992.

By air: The ultra-modern **Aeroport del Prat** is located south-west of the city, 25 minutes away from the centre by taxi. A range of countries is also served from **Madrid**, with good internal connections to Barcelona. Charter flights from London and other European cities operate into **Reus** on the Costa Dorada to the south of the city, mainly to access the coastal resorts and the Port Aventura theme park. Barcelona is a day trip from Reus by car or train. For flight information and reservations, **Iberia Airlines** of Spain, ☎ 93 412-7020 or 93 412-4748.

By road: The city is connected to the French border (1½ hours away) and to the rest of Spain via the motorway (*auto-pista*). Travelling in Catalunya by road is easy; Girona, Tarragona and Valencia are all accessible via the motorway. Other roads include *autovias* (dual carriageways) and *carretera estatal*, all good main roads. If you bring your own car into the country and live outside the EC, a **Green Card** is necessary; third party insurance is compulsory. An **international driving licence** is also required. Driving in Spain is on the right. Hiring a car for a stay in Barcelona, however, is not necessary as the city's public transport system is so efficient. In order to hire a car, drivers must be over 21 with a year's driving experience. Don't leave anything in your car because vehicle crime is a problem. Road conditions and travel information are available in Spanish on the **Teleruta** service, ☎ 91 535-2222.

Speed limits are 120 kph (75 mph) on *autopistas*, 120, 100 or 80 according to signs on *autovias*, 90 on country roads and 60 on urban roads. Stiff, on-the-spot speeding fines are not uncommon. Wearing of seatbelts is compulsory in the front and if fitted, in the back. **Motorcyclists** must wear safety helmets by law.

Buses: operate to Barcelona from Bilbao, Andorra, Costa Brava, Cordoba, Grenada, Seville, Madrid, San Sebastian, Girona and many other Spanish and international cities. There are several different companies, each featuring different destinations. The best way to find out what's on offer is to call in at the **Estacio del Nord**, Avinguda Vilanova, ☎ 93 265-6508. For buses between Barcelona and the Costa Brava, call Empresa Sarfa on ☎ 93 318-9735.

By rail: Estacio-Sants is the city's main railway station, with trains linking Barcelona to the rest of Spain and Europe. There are several types of trains: RENFE is the national rail company and trains vary from *Pendular* (the fastest inter-city services), *Talgo* and *Electrotren* to *Expreso* and *Rapido* (ironically the slowest, regional services). English is spoken at the RENFE office at Sants.

By boat: Ferries to the Balearic Islands leave regularly from Barcelona's Estacio Maritima at the end of La Rambla, and are operated by Trasmediterranea, ☎ 93 412-2524. Book in advance during summer.

What to Pack

If you plan to take advantage of Barcelona's nightlife, **high fashion** is essential! This is a cosmopolitan city and you can never be overdressed. Otherwise, **casual wear** is fine for sightseeing. Remember sunglasses and a hat for summer, comfortable shoes for walking around the city, and **smart casual** for the evenings. Some restaurants will expect jacket and tie and people dress up for the opera. Show respect when entering the cathedral or churches, or visiting Montserrat – women should wear long skirts and cover their shoulders and men should not wear shorts. Some of the smarter hotels have pools so bring swimming gear. Otherwise, Barcelona sells everything you could buy in any other big city.

Money Matters

Spain is one of the members of the European Union and the **currency** is now the Euro. There are **banks** and **exchange bureaux** all over the city, some of which take overseas credit cards in their automatic tellers; banking hours are ⊕ 09:00–14:00 Monday–Friday and 09:00–13:00 on Saturdays, although they vary occasionally. All major **credit cards** are accepted although some country restaurants and small tapas bars may require cash. Holders of cards bearing the Visa,

Flamenco

Though not especially Catalan, flamenco is performed in a number of clubs around the city. An outlet for passion and unhappiness, good flamenco is a spiritual bond between dancer, musicians and onlookers, as the emotion of the song, the hypnotic hand-clapping and finger-snapping of the audience and the fantastically fast stamping of the dancer build up to a finale accompanied by spontaneous shouts of encouragement and emotion.

Strands of many cultures have come together to form the music as we know it today, but it originates from the gypsies of Seville, Jerez and Cadiz in the 19th century, who sang mournful laments of lost love and oppression.

Mastercard, Cirrus and Plus signs can use Spanish automatic tellers, which have instructions in English. A fee is always charged for this.

Traveller's cheques can be changed in banks and the Bureaux de Change which operate in the main resorts.

Foreign banks in Barcelona include a Barclays, Chase Manhattan and NatWest on the Passeig de Gràcia; Bank of America on carrer Bori i Fontesta, and Lloyds Bank on the Rambla de Catalunya and the Diagonal. The exchange bureau at the airport is open ⏰ 07:45–10:45.

Spanish **sales tax** (IVA) is currently 16% and is not always included in the price, so be aware of this when you make a purchase.

Tipping is optional; around 10% of the price of a meal is acceptable. Petrol pump attendants and taxi drivers also expect a small tip.

Transport

Barcelona has an excellent **Metro** system, easy to use, clean, regular and relatively safe. The best value is a block of 10 tickets which gives considerable savings over 10 singles. Local women do seem quite nervous on the Metro at night, so tourists should follow their example and always sit with other people. Guard your belongings and after about 21:00 or towards the end of the lines, take a taxi instead. Barcelona's 11,000 **taxis** are convenient and not particularly expensive. They can be hailed on the street or found at taxi ranks. A green light on the top means the taxi is available. Drivers tend not to speak English but all taxis are metered so communication is rarely a problem. There's an extra tax for travel with large pieces of luggage. Tips are appreciated but not expected.

Buses run throughout the city and a special tourist bus operates in summer, the Bus 100 or **Bus Turístic**. During summer, from mid-June to mid-October, the Bus Turístic runs on two circular routes, stopping (26 stops in all) at the main places of interest in the city. The ticket is valid all day and allows passengers to get on and off the bus for as many times and for as long as they want, as well as obtain major discounts on some visits. The ticket is purchased on board. Service starts and ends at Plaça Catalunya. In addition, there's an **antique tram** (Tramvia Bleu) running from Tibidabo train stop to a funicular railway which travels to the top of the mountain. **Cable cars** operate from the top of Montjuïc to the harbour and on to Barceloneta. A second, underground funicular connects the Paral.lel metro station

to Montjuïc, emerging within walking distance of the Joan Miró foundation and the amusement park. **Trains** leave Sants railway station for Sitges every half an hour. The **Sitges** station, behind the town, is about 20 minutes from the beach. Getting to **Montserrat** is easy. **FF.CC** trains (commuter trains – Ferrocarils de la Generalitat de Catalunya) regularly depart from the Plaça d'Espanya heading for Manresa. Leave the train at the Montserrat Aeri stop and take the cable car, which runs every 15 minutes, to the monastery. One of the best ways to travel up the **Costa Brava**, just 60km (37½ miles) to the north, is by **boat**. Crucero boats depart from **Lloret de Mar**, the first big resort, calling at most of the major ports to the north. For information and a schedule, ☎ 972 36-4499.

Business Hours

Shops and businesses are generally open ☺ 09:00 or 10:00 to 13:30 or 14:00 and close for a siesta. They reopen 16:00–20:00. Some businesses start much earlier, around 08:00 and work straight through to 15:00 with no siesta. Hours also change in the summer. Big department stores now stay open all day but most supermarkets close for lunch. In the resorts, the souvenir shops are open as late as 22:00 in summer. Lunch tends to be served from about 13:00 to 16:00, with dinner from 20:00 (sometimes earlier for the benefit of the tourists) to 24:00. Bars and clubs stay open late on the coast – sometimes until 04:00.

Time Difference

Spain is GMT+1 hour in winter and GMT+2 hours from the last Sunday in March to the last Sunday in October in summer.

Communications

The international dialling code for Spain is ☎ +34 9. Each province has its own dialling prefix. The number for Barcelona is ☎ +34 93 when dialling from overseas or ☎ 93 when dialling from within Spain or Barcelona itself. Full instructions on the use of public telephones are shown in English in the kiosk. Cheap rates are between 22:00 and 08:00. To call overseas, dial ☎ 00 and wait for the tone to change before dialling the country code and the number. **Telephone cards** can be bought from Telefónica offices or tobacconists. **Mobile phones** operate on 1800 and 900 MHZ frequencies, with comprehensive coverage.

The main, very grand **post office** (*Correos*) is at the end of the Passeig de Colom on Placa d'Antoni Lopez; ☉ open 08:30–22:00 Monday–Saturday and 10:00–12:00 Sunday. There's a poste restante service here. Stamps can be bought from tobacconists or from hotel receptions.

Electricity

The power system is 220 or 225 volts AC. Older buildings occasionally have 110 or 125 volts AC and should be treated with extreme caution. Two-pin **plugs** are used. Americans will need a transformer, British visitors an adaptor.

Weights and Measures

Spain uses the metric system.

Health Precautions

An excess of sun and sangría are the worst problems encountered by most people. Use a high-factor sun protection cream, wear a hat and take special care in the height of summer. Drink bottled water if you get a stomach upset. A mosquito repellant is also a good idea.

Health Services

Spanish pharmacists are highly trained and they can dispense medicines often only available on prescription; ☉ opening hours are 09:00–13:30 and 17:00–20:30 (with the occasional half-hour variation). Every area has a duty pharmacy with a 24-hour service, the address of which is displayed on the doors of other pharmacies.

Personal Safety

Petty crime is the only problem travellers are likely to face, though the Barri Gòtic, Barri Xines, Barceloneta and La Ribera are better avoided at night. Don't leave anything in a car; be careful with wallets; watch out for pickpockets on La Rambla; don't wear ostentatious jewellery and use hotel safe deposit boxes. Some inland areas are very poor, so bag snatching is a temptation. Sexual harassment is not generally a problem and as the city streets are usually busy at night, women travellers should feel safe walking around the resorts. Be alert if travelling by metro, particularly if you're a single woman.

Emergencies

Policia Nacional: **091**
Policia Municipal: **092**
Emergency Medical Service: **061** Police Assistance (Tourist Attention), ☎ 93 301-9060. The tourist police station, ✉ Rambla 43, is open ⏱ 24 hours a day in the summer.

Etiquette

Topless sunbathing is acceptable on the beaches but more modesty is appropriate inland around lakes and in the national parks. Visitors are advised to adopt the Spanish siesta routine; visiting sights and expecting to have meetings during the early afternoon is not appropriate. Expect to have dinner late; most Spaniards only eat at 22:00 or 23:00 in the summer, but earlier in the winter.

Language

Catalan is today the main language spoken by 10 million people worldwide. Many of its derivations are French and the written word looks like a mixture of French and Spanish. The spoken word, however, is harsher sounding than French or Spanish and some accents outside the city are very strong. Most signs and maps are now in Catalan, although some are in **Castilian** as well. Castilian speakers will still be understood as virtually all Catalans are bilingual. Business can be conducted in either language. **English** is also understood in business circles and by people working in service industries, although sign language may be necessary in some smaller shops, markets and in taxis.

Catalan Phrases
Si, No, Val •
Yes, No, OK
Si us plau, Gràcies
(*Merci* in north Catalunya) • Please, Thank you
Hola, Adéu •
Hello, Goodbye
Bona tarde/nit • Good afternoon/night
¿Com va? •
How are you?
(No) ho entenc •
I (don't) understand
¿Parleu anglés? • Do you speak English?
Em dic • My name is
Es massa car • It's too expensive
¿On és? • Where is?
¿Qué hi ha per menjar? • What is there to eat?

Barcelona for Free
Travelling on a budget is rewarding in Barcelona as many of the attractions are free. You can visit the Olympic Stadium; peer into the cool depths of the cathedral; admire the buildings and the Parc Güell by Gaudí; inspect the museums of graphic art, coins, ethnography and perfume; poke around the Boquería market, enjoy the street entertainment in La Rambla; and window shop in the design emporium Vinçon, virtually a museum in itself.

INDEX OF SIGHTS

General Index

GENERAL INDEX